The Sainsbury Book of
FREEZING
Gill Edden

CONTENTS

Published exclusively for
J Sainsbury Limited
Stamford Street, London SE1 9LL
by Cathay Books
59 Grosvenor Street, London W1

First Published 1980

© Cathay Books 1980
ISBN 0 86178 46 9

Printed in Hong Kong

INTRODUCTION

The freezer has many advantages to offer. It enables you to preserve home-grown produce and cheap seasonal foods. It can also provide a store of ready-cooked meals. Cook at your leisure and save time too: prepare double the recipe quantities and freeze both portions, or keep one aside for the next meal.

Packaging: For successful freezing, packaging is most important to prevent dehydration. When rigid containers are required, use strong foil dishes or polythene containers. Only heavy duty polythene bags are suitable for freezing. Similarly, heavy duty foil and plastic wrap, usually called 'freezer foil' and 'freezer wrap', should be used; these must always be over-wrapped with a polythene bag to prevent puncturing. Containers must be properly sealed. Use wire twist ties or freezer tape for sealing bags and squeeze as much air out of a pack as possible before sealing.

Storage Times: All of the cooked dishes in this book can be stored in the freezer for up to 3 months, although they are generally at their best if eaten within 2 months of freezing.

Other points to remember: The consistency of a sauce is inclined to change in the freezer, so thicken after thawing if possible. Seasonings sometimes become more concentrated, so under-season slightly before freezing and adjust before serving. Finally, do be sure meat and poultry are thoroughly heated through before serving.

NOTES

Standard spoon measurements are used in all recipes
1 tablespoon = one 15 ml spoon
1 teaspoon = one 5 ml spoon
All spoon measures are level.

Fresh herbs are used unless otherwise stated. If unobtainable, substitute a bouquet garni of the equivalent dried herbs, or use dried herbs instead but halve the quantities stated.

Use freshly ground black pepper where pepper is specified.

If fresh yeast is unobtainable, substitute dried yeast but use only half the recommended quantity and follow the manufacturer's instructions for reconstituting.

Ovens should be preheated to the specified temperature.

For all recipes, quantities are given in both metric and imperial measures. Follow either set but not a mixture of both, because they are not inter-changeable.

SOUPS & SAUCES

Carrot Soup

25 g (1 oz) butter
500 g (1 lb) carrots,
   sliced
1 onion, sliced
1 clove garlic, crushed
1 litre (1¾ pints)
   chicken stock
salt and pepper
TO SERVE:
1 tablespoon cornflour,
   blended with
      2 tablespoons water
2 teaspoons chopped
   mint
mint sprigs
croûtons

Melt the butter in a large pan. Add the carrots, onion and garlic and cook gently until soft. Add the stock and salt and pepper to taste. Bring to the boil and simmer for about 25 minutes. Purée in an electric blender or rub through a sieve. Cool.

TO FREEZE: Pour into a rigid container, seal, label and freeze.

TO SERVE: Turn into a saucepan and heat gently until thawed. Stir in the blended cornflour and bring to the boil. Simmer, stirring, until slightly thickened, then stir in the chopped mint. Garnish with mint and serve with croûtons.

Serves 4 to 6

Country Vegetable Soup

50 g (2 oz) butter
1 onion, chopped
2 carrots, chopped
2 celery sticks,
    chopped
1 large potato,
    chopped
1 x 227 g (8 oz) can
    tomatoes
600 ml (1 pint) beef
    stock
1 teaspoon tomato
    purée
salt and pepper
TO SERVE:
chopped chives or
    celery leaves

Melt the butter in a large pan, add the vegetables and cook until soft. Chop the tomatoes and add to the pan with their juice, the stock, tomato purée and salt and pepper to taste. Bring to the boil, cover and simmer for 30 minutes.

Remove from the heat, cool slightly, then purée in an electric blender or rub through a sieve. Cool.

TO FREEZE: Pour into a rigid container, seal, label and freeze.

TO SERVE: Turn into a saucepan and heat gently until thawed. Bring to the boil and simmer for 5 minutes. Check the seasoning. Serve garnished with chives or celery leaves.

Serves 6

Game Soup

2 tablespoons oil
1 pigeon
1 onion, finely
    chopped
2 carrots, finely
    chopped
2 celery sticks, finely
    sliced
1 tablespoon
    cornflour
4 mushrooms,
    chopped
900 ml (1½ pints)
    beef stock
salt and pepper

Heat the oil in a large pan. Brown the pigeon on all sides then remove.

Add the onion, carrot and celery to the pan and fry until lightly browned. Stir in the cornflour and cook for 1 to 2 minutes, stirring.

Return the pigeon to the pan with the mushrooms, stock and salt and pepper to taste. Bring to the boil, cover and simmer for about 1 hour.

Chop the meat from the pigeon, finely and return to the soup. Cool.

TO FREEZE: Pour into a rigid container, seal, label and freeze.

TO SERVE: Turn into a saucepan and thaw over gentle heat, then bring to the boil, cover and simmer for 10 minutes, stirring occasionally. Check the seasoning before serving.

Serves 4 to 6

Cream of Mushroom Soup

50 g (2 oz) butter
1 small onion,
    chopped
250 g (8 oz)
    mushrooms,
    chopped
salt and pepper
25 g (1 oz) plain
    flour
450 ml (¾ pint)
    chicken stock
TO SERVE:
3-4 mushrooms,
    sliced and sauteed
    in a little butter
150 ml (¼ pint)
    milk
150 ml (¼ pint)
    single cream

Melt 25 g (1 oz) of the butter in a pan. Add the onion and cook gently, stirring, until softened. Add the chopped mushrooms, with a little salt and pepper. Cook until softened.

Melt the remaining 25 g (1 oz) butter in another pan. Stir in the flour and cook, stirring, for 1 to 2 minutes. Gradually stir in the stock and bring to the boil. Cook, stirring, for 2 to 3 minutes, then add the mushrooms and onions. Purée the soup in an electric blender, or rub through a sieve. Cool.

TO FREEZE: Pour into a rigid container, seal, label and freeze.

TO SERVE: Turn into a saucepan and heat gently until thawed.

Bring to the boil, then stir in the milk and cream. Check the seasoning. Heat through without boiling. Serve garnished with the mushrooms.

Serves 4

Minestrone

2 tablespoons oil
1 carrot, chopped
1 onion, chopped
2 celery sticks,
   chopped
1.2 litres (2 pints)
   chicken stock
1 bay leaf
1 leek, shredded
1 potato, chopped
1 x 227 g (8 oz) can
   tomatoes
1 clove garlic, crushed
¼ cauliflower,
   broken into florets
75 g (3 oz) pasta
   shells
salt and pepper
TO SERVE:
grated Parmesan
   cheese

Heat the oil in a large pan. Add the carrot, onion and celery and fry until just beginning to colour. Add the stock, bay leaf, leek and potato. Bring to the boil, cover and simmer for about 40 minutes.

Chop the tomatoes and add to the pan with their juice, the garlic, cauliflower, pasta and salt and pepper to taste. Simmer for 12 to 15 minutes, until the pasta is tender. Cool.

TO FREEZE: Pour into a rigid container, seal, label and freeze.

TO SERVE: Turn into a saucepan and heat gently until thawed, then bring to the boil, cover and simmer for 5 minutes. Check the seasoning, spoon into individual soup bowls and sprinkle with the cheese.
Serves 6

Oxtail Soup

25 g (1 oz) beef
   dripping
1 oxtail, chopped
1 large onion,
   chopped
1 carrot, chopped
1 celery stick,
   chopped
2.25 litres (4 pints)
   beef stock
bouquet garni
salt and pepper
TO SERVE:
1 tablespoon cornflour,
   blended with
   2 tablespoons water
2 tablespoons sherry

Melt the dripping in a pan, add the oxtail and fry until well browned. Remove from the pan, add the vegetables and sauté until soft. Return the oxtail to the pan, add the stock, bouquet garni and salt and pepper to taste. Bring to the boil, cover and simmer for 3 to 4 hours until tender.

Strain the soup. Remove the meat from the bones, shred finely and set aside with the vegetables. Cool the liquid, chill, then skim off the fat layer and return the meat and vegetables to the soup.

TO FREEZE: Spoon into a rigid container, seal, label and freeze.

TO SERVE: Turn into a saucepan and heat gently until thawed. Bring to the boil, cover and simmer for 15 minutes. Stir in the blended cornflour and simmer, stirring, for 2 minutes. Add the sherry and check the seasoning.

Serves 6

Cream of Haddock Soup

50 g (2 oz) butter
1 onion, sliced
1 carrot, sliced
1 celery stick, sliced
1 bay leaf
6 peppercorns
1 lemon slice
120 ml (4 fl oz) dry
  vermouth
900 ml (1½ pints)
  water
salt
500 g (1 lb) filleted
  haddock
3 tablespoons plain
  flour
TO SERVE:
125 g (4 oz) frozen
  peeled prawns,
  thawed
4 tablespoons single
  cream
chervil or parsley

Melt 15 g (½ oz) of the butter in a large saucepan and sauté the onion until soft. Add the carrot, celery, bay leaf, peppercorns, lemon, vermouth, water and salt to taste. Bring to the boil, cover and simmer for 20 minutes. Strain.

Poach the fish gently in 200 ml (⅓ pint) of the stock for 10 minutes, then remove and cool.

Melt the remaining butter in a pan, stir in the flour and cook, stirring, for 2 to 3 minutes. Gradually stir in the remaining stock. Bring to the boil and simmer, uncovered, for 10 minutes.

Return the fish to the soup and purée in an electric blender or rub through a sieve. Cool.

TO FREEZE: Pour into a rigid container, seal, label and freeze.

TO SERVE: Turn into a saucepan. Heat gently until thawed, then bring to the boil, stirring. Add the prawns, check the seasoning and simmer for a few minutes. Stir in the cream and garnish with chervil or parsley.
Serves 6

Tomato and Pepper Sauce

4 tablespoons oil
4 onions, chopped
2 large green
    peppers, chopped
2 x 397 g (14 oz)
    cans tomatoes
salt and pepper
2 teaspoons
    Worcestershire
    sauce
1 bay leaf
TO SERVE (optional):
1 tablespoon cornflour,
    blended with
    2 tablespoons water

Heat the oil in a pan, add the onion and green pepper and fry until soft. Add the tomatoes with their juice, salt and pepper to taste, Worcestershire sauce and bay leaf. Simmer for about 30 minutes, until reduced to a thick pulp. Cool.

TO FREEZE: Pour into small rigid containers, seal, label and freeze.

TO SERVE: Turn into a saucepan and heat gently until thawed. If a thick sauce is required, stir in the blended cornflour and bring to the boil; simmer, stirring, until thickened.
    Serve with meat, fish or pasta.
Makes about 1.2 litres (2 pints)

Rich Brown Sauce

3 tablespoons oil
1 onion, chopped
1 carrot, finely
    chopped
1 celery stick, finely
    chopped
40 g (1½ oz) plain
    flour
2 teaspoons tomato
    purée
2 mushrooms,
    chopped
1.2 litres (2 pints)
    jellied beef stock
bouquet garni
2 shallots, finely
    chopped
250 ml (8 fl oz) red
    wine
rosemary sprig
small piece of lemon
    rind
salt and pepper
TO SERVE (optional):
1 tablespoon cornflour,
    blended with
    2 tablespoons water

Heat the oil in a pan. Add the onion, carrot and celery and fry until just beginning to brown. Add the flour and cook, stirring, until golden, then add the tomato purée, mushrooms, stock and bouquet garni. Bring to the boil, cover and simmer for 30 minutes, skimming occasionally.
    Meanwhile, put the shallots in a small pan with the wine, rosemary and lemon rind. Bring to the boil and boil until reduced by about half. Discard the rosemary and lemon rind. Add the wine and shallots to the sauce and season with salt and pepper to taste. Simmer for 10 minutes, skimming occasionally. Strain and cool.

TO FREEZE: Pour into small rigid containers, seal, label and freeze.

TO SERVE: Turn into a saucepan and thaw over gentle heat. Bring to the boil and simmer for 2 to 3 minutes. If a thicker sauce is required, add the blended cornflour and simmer, stirring until thickened.
Makes about 1.2 litres (2 pints)

Bolognese Sauce

500 g (1 lb) minced
    beef
2 onions, chopped
2 cloves garlic,
    crushed
1 x 397 g (14 oz)
    can tomatoes
1 x 65 g (2¼ oz)
    can tomato purée
2 teaspoons each dried
    basil and oregano
2 bay leaves
salt and pepper
TO SERVE:
1 tablespoon cornflour,
    blended with
    2 tablespoons water
grated Parmesan
    cheese (optional)

Put the beef in a large pan and cook over gentle heat, stirring, until browned. Add the onions and cook, stirring, until soft. Add the remaining ingredients, with salt and pepper to taste. Bring to the boil, cover and simmer for about 45 minutes, stirring occasionally. Discard the bay leaves and cool.

TO FREEZE: Spoon into a rigid container, seal, label and freeze.

TO SERVE: Turn into a saucepan and heat gently until thawed, stirring occasionally. Bring to the boil, cover and simmer for 20 minutes, stirring occasionally.

Add the blended cornflour and simmer, stirring, for 2 to 3 minutes until thickened. Serve with pasta; top with Parmesan cheese if preferred.

Serves 4 to 6

Barbecue Sauce

50 g (2 oz) streaky
    bacon, derinded
    and chopped
1 onion, chopped
1 green pepper,
    chopped
25 g (1 oz) plain
    flour
1 x 397 g (14 oz)
    can tomatoes
1 clove garlic, crushed
1 teaspoon chilli
    seasoning
1 teaspoon paprika
1 teaspoon soy sauce
300 ml (½ pint)
    stock
salt and pepper

Fry the bacon gently in a dry frying pan until the fat runs, then add the onion and pepper and cook, stirring, until soft. Add the flour and cook, stirring, for 1 to 2 minutes.

Add the remaining ingredients, with salt and pepper to taste. Bring to the boil, cover and simmer for about 25 minutes, stirring occasionally. Cool.

TO FREEZE: Pour into rigid containers, seal, label and freeze.

TO SERVE: Turn into a saucepan and thaw over gentle heat. Bring to the boil and simmer for 2 to 3 minutes.

Makes about 900 ml (1½ pints)

Salsa Venezia

25 g (1 oz) butter
1 onion, chopped
1 clove garlic, crushed
125 g (4 oz)
    mushrooms, sliced
500 g (1 lb) tomatoes,
    skinned and chopped
2 teaspoons tomato
    purée
½ teaspoon each
    dried basil and
    marjoram
3 tablespoons dry
    vermouth
2 tablespoons lemon
    juice
salt and pepper
500 g (1 lb) peeled
    prawns
1 tablespoon cornflour
2 tablespoons oil
TO SERVE:
2 teaspoons cornflour,
    blended with
    1 tablespoon water

Melt the butter in a pan. Add the onion and garlic and cook until soft and transparent. Add the mushrooms and cook until soft, then stir in the tomatoes, tomato purée, herbs, vermouth, lemon juice and a little salt and pepper.

Toss the prawns in the cornflour until evenly coated. Heat the oil in a pan, add the prawns and fry gently until golden. Stir into the sauce and simmer for about 5 minutes, stirring. Cool.

TO FREEZE: Spoon into a rigid container, seal, label and freeze.

TO SERVE: Turn into a saucepan and thaw over gentle heat, stirring occasionally, then cover and simmer for about 15 minutes. Stir in the blended cornflour and simmer, stirring, for 4 to 5 minutes. Check the seasoning and serve with pasta.

Serves 4 to 6

Béchamel Sauce

1.2 litres (2 pints)
 milk
½ onion
½ carrot
1-2 parsley sprigs
1-2 thyme sprigs
2 bay leaves
2-3 blades mace
6 peppercorns
½ teaspoon salt
50 g (2 oz) butter
50 g (2 oz) plain
 flour

Put the milk in a saucepan with the onion, carrot, herbs and seasonings. Heat gently just to scalding point, then remove from the heat, cover and leave to infuse for 20 minutes; strain.

Melt the butter in a pan, add the flour and cook, stirring, for 2 minutes. Remove from the heat and stir in the milk. Return to the heat and cook, stirring, for 5 minutes. Cool.

TO FREEZE: Pour into rigid containers, seal, label and freeze.

TO SERVE: Turn into a saucepan and heat gently until thawed. Bring to the boil, stirring, then simmer, stirring, for 1 to 2 minutes.

Serve with vegetables or fish, or use as a basis for other sauces.

Makes 1.2 litres (2 pints)

Rich Chocolate Sauce

4 sugar lumps
1 orange
75 g (3 oz)
 granulated sugar
300 ml (½ pint)
 water
175 g (6 oz) plain
 chocolate, in pieces

Rub the lumps of sugar over the orange rind to soak up the flavour and colour. Place in a pan with the granulated sugar and water and heat gently, stirring, until the sugar is dissolved. Bring to the boil and boil for 5 minutes without stirring. Remove from the heat.

Add the chocolate, stir until melted, then beat well. Return to the heat and simmer until the sauce is syrupy. Cool.

TO FREEZE: Pour into a rigid container, seal, label and freeze.

TO SERVE: Thaw at room temperature for 2 to 3 hours. Serve cold with ice cream or profiteroles, or heat gently, stirring, to serve with puddings.

Makes about 450 ml (¾ pint)

Raspberry and Redcurrant Sauce

500 g (1 lb)
*   redcurrants*
2 tablespoons water
125 g (4 oz) caster
*   sugar*
500 g (1 lb)
*   raspberries*

Put the redcurrants in a pan with the water and sugar. Heat gently until the sugar is dissolved, then simmer until the fruit is soft. Add the raspberries and leave until cool.

Purée the fruit mixture in an electric blender then strain, or rub through a sieve.

TO FREEZE: Pour into rigid containers, seal, label and freeze.

TO SERVE: Thaw at room temperature for 3 to 4 hours. Serve cold with ice cream, or heat gently to serve with puddings.

Makes about 900 ml (1½ pints)

FISH

Cod à la Provençale

25 g (1 oz) flour
salt and pepper
750 g (1½ lb) cod
  fillets, skinned
3 tablespoons oil
2 onions, sliced
1 clove garlic,
  crushed
1 tablespoon chopped
  parsley
300 ml (½ pint)
  tomato juice
2 tablespoons lemon
  juice
TO SERVE:
125 g (4 oz) frozen
  peeled prawns,
  thawed

Season the flour with salt and pepper and use to coat the fish fillets. Heat the oil in a pan, add the fish and fry until golden, then place in a foil dish. Add the onions to the pan and fry until coloured. Spoon over the fish. Blend the garlic and parsley with the tomato and lemon juices and pour over the fish. Cool.

TO FREEZE: Cover, place in a polythene bag, seal, label and freeze.

TO SERVE: Uncover and place in a preheated moderately hot oven, 190°C (375°F), Gas Mark 5, for about 30 minutes. Stir in the prawns, cover loosely with foil and cook for about 15 minutes. Check the seasoning before serving.

Serves 4

Sole au Gratin

4 large sole fillets
salt and pepper
1 tablespoon lemon
    juice
300 ml (½ pint)
    water
300 ml (½ pint)
    Béchamel sauce
    (see page 16),
    cooled
TO SERVE:
2 tablespoons dried
    breadcrumbs

Place the fillets in a single layer in a roasting pan. Sprinkle with salt, pepper and lemon juice and add the water. Cook in a preheated moderate oven, 180°C (350°F), Gas Mark 4, for about 10 minutes. Drain and cool.

TO FREEZE: Transfer the fish to a shallow foil dish and spoon the Béchamel sauce over the top. Cover, place in a polythene bag, seal, label and freeze.

TO SERVE: Uncover, sprinkle with breadcrumbs and reheat from frozen in a preheated moderate oven, 180°C (350°F), Gas Mark 4, for about 30 minutes.

Serves 4

Mushroom-Stuffed Plaice

50 g (2 oz) butter
½ onion, chopped
50 g (2 oz) mush-
rooms, chopped
50 g (2 oz) fresh
breadcrumbs
2 tablespoons
chopped parsley
1 tablespoon grated
lemon rind
1 tablespoon lemon
juice
salt and pepper
1 egg, beaten
8 plaice fillets
TO SERVE:
2 tablespoons fresh
breadcrumbs
2 tablespoons grated
Parmesan cheese
parsley sprigs

Melt the butter in a small frying pan, add the onion and cook until soft. Add the mushrooms and breadcrumbs and cook until the crumbs are golden. Remove from the heat and stir in the parsley, lemon rind, lemon juice and salt and pepper to taste. Bind with egg. Cool.

Divide the mixture between the fillets, placing it on the wide end of the fish, and fold the tail end over. Place in a greased foil dish.

TO FREEZE: Cover, place in a polythene bag, seal, label and freeze.

TO SERVE: Unwrap, sprinkle with breadcrumbs and cheese and cook from frozen in a preheated moderately hot oven, 190°C (375°F), Gas Mark 5, for 30 to 35 minutes. Garnish with parsley.
Serves 4

Fish and Potato Pie

250 g (8 oz) cod
fillet
salt and pepper
300 ml (½ pint)
milk
50 g (2 oz) butter
25 g (1 oz) plain
flour
1 tablespoon lemon
juice
pinch of paprika
500 g (1 lb)
potatoes, cooked
125 g (4 oz) peeled
prawns
TO SERVE:
parsley sprigs

Put the cod in a pan, sprinkle with salt and pepper and add the milk. Bring to the boil and poach for about 5 minutes. Drain, reserving the cooking liquid, and leave to cool.

Melt half the butter in another pan, stir in the flour and cook for 2 to 3 minutes. Remove from the heat and blend in the reserved liquid. Add the lemon juice and paprika. Cool.

Cream the potatoes with the remaining butter.

TO FREEZE: Flake the cod and place in a foil dish with the prawns. Pour over the sauce and smooth the potato over the top. Cover, place in a polythene bag, seal, label and freeze.

TO SERVE: Uncover and reheat from frozen in a preheated moderately hot oven, 190°C (375°F), Gas Mark 5, for about 1 hour. Garnish with parsley.
Serves 4

Halibut Basquaise

750 g (1½ lb)
  halibut fillet
1 tablespoon lemon
  juice
salt and pepper
3 tablespoons olive
  oil
4 onions, sliced
2 cloves garlic,
  crushed
2 teaspoons tomato
  purée
2 teaspoons paprika
pinch of cayenne
  pepper
pinch of ground mace
250 ml (8 fl oz) red
  wine
120 ml (4 fl oz)
  water
TO SERVE:
2 teaspoons cornflour,
  blended with
  1 tablespoon water
4 slices fried bread
lemon wedges

Put the fish in a buttered ovenproof dish. Sprinkle with the lemon juice and salt and pepper to taste, cover and poach in a preheated moderate oven, 180°C (350°F), Gas Mark 4, for about 15 minutes. Drain and cool.

Heat the oil in a pan. Add the onions and garlic and cook gently until softened. Add the tomato purée, paprika, cayenne and mace. Stir in the wine and water and bring to the boil. Simmer, uncovered, for 10 to 15 minutes. Cool.

TO FREEZE: Cut the halibut into 4 portions and arrange in a foil dish. Spoon the sauce over the top. Cover, place in a polythene bag, seal, label and freeze.

TO SERVE: Unwrap, cover loosely with foil, then reheat from frozen in a preheated moderately hot oven, 190°C (375°F), Gas Mark 5, for 45 minutes. Stir in the cornflour, then return to the oven for 10 minutes.

Serve the fish and sauce on the fried bread, with lemon wedges.
Serves 4

Haddock Croquettes

500 g (1 lb) haddock
  fillet
6 peppercorns
1 tablespoon lemon
  juice
2 tablespoons water
salt and pepper
350 g (12 oz)
  potatoes, cooked
25 g (1 oz) butter
2 eggs, beaten
  separately
flour for coating
50 g (2 oz) fresh
  white breadcrumbs
TO SERVE:
oil for deep frying
parsley sprigs
  Tomato and Pepper
    Sauce (see page
    12) or tartare
    sauce

Cut the haddock into 4 pieces and
place in a buttered pan. Add the
peppercorns, lemon juice, water and
salt to taste. Cover and cook gently
for about 15 minutes until the fish
flakes easily. Cool.

Press the potatoes through a sieve
into a large basin. Remove the skin
and any bones from the haddock,
then flake. Add to the potato, mix
well, then beat in the butter and
season with salt and pepper to taste.
Add 1 egg, mix thoroughly and chill.

Shape heaped tablespoonfuls of the
mixture into croquettes on a floured
board. Dip in the remaining egg and
coat with breadcrumbs.

TO FREEZE: Place on a tray and freeze
unwrapped, then pack in a polythene
bag, seal, label and return to the
freezer.

TO SERVE: Unwrap and place on a
tray. Thaw at room temperature for
about 3 hours, then deep fry in the
hot oil until golden brown.

Garnish with parsley and serve
with Tomato and Pepper Sauce or
tartare sauce.
Serves 4

Fish Balls

500 g (1 lb) haddock
   fillet
salt and pepper
1 tablespoon lemon
   juice
250 g (8 oz)
   potatoes
bunch of watercress
2 eggs, beaten
   separately
25 g (1 oz) plain
   flour
50 g (2 oz) dry
   breadcrumbs
TO SERVE:
oil for deep frying
watercress sprigs

Place the haddock in a greased ovenproof dish. Season with salt and pepper to taste and sprinkle with lemon juice. Cover and bake in a preheated moderate oven, 180°C (350°F), Gas Mark 4, for about 10 minutes, until the fish is just opaque.

Meanwhile, cook the potatoes with the watercress in boiling salted water until the potatoes are tender.

Drain the fish, discard the skin and mash the fish with a fork.

Drain the potatoes and watercress and press through a sieve into a bowl. Add the fish and salt and pepper to taste. Bind the mixture with 1 egg. Chill for 15 minutes.

Shape heaped teaspoonfuls of the mixture into balls. Coat with flour, then dip in the remaining egg and coat with breadcrumbs.

TO FREEZE: Place on a tray and freeze unwrapped, then pack in a polythene bag, seal, label, return to the freezer.

TO SERVE: Unwrap and place on a tray. Thaw at room temperature for about 3 hours, then deep fry in the hot oil until golden brown. Garnish with watercress.

Serves 4

Salmon Mousse

1 x 205 g (7½ oz)
    can red salmon
salt and pepper
1 tablespoon sherry
300 ml (½ pint)
    Béchamel Sauce
    (see page 16)
3 tablespoons
    whipped cream
TO SERVE:
shredded Chinese
    cabbage leaves
sliced radishes
chopped cucumber

Drain and flake the salmon, add salt and pepper to taste and the sherry. Stir in the cooled sauce, then work in an electric blender for about 30 seconds until smooth. Turn into a basin. Fold in the cream. Spoon into freezerproof ramekin dishes and chill.
TO FREEZE: Cover each dish with foil, place them all in a polythene bag, seal, label and freeze.
TO SERVE: Thaw, covered, in the refrigerator for about 8 hours. Top with cabbage, radish and cucumber.
Serves 4

Curried Fish Tartlets

PASTRY:
150 g (5 oz) plain
    flour
pinch of salt
40 g (1½ oz) lard
25 g (1 oz) butter
4-6 teaspoons water
FILLING:
250 g (8 oz)
    haddock fillet
25 g (1 oz) butter
1 small onion, finely
    chopped
1 teaspoon curry
    powder
25 g (1 oz) plain
    flour
150 ml (¼ pint)
    milk
1 egg, beaten
salt and pepper
TO SERVE:
chopped fennel

Sift the flour and salt into a bowl and rub in the fat. Mix in enough water to give a firm dough. Knead lightly, place in a polythene bag and chill for 30 minutes.
    Roll out the pastry thinly, cut out 6 circles and use to line patty tins.
    Poach the haddock in water to cover for 10 minutes. Drain, cool, then flake, discarding any skin.
    Melt the butter in a pan, add the onion and cook for 2 to 3 minutes, until softened. Add the curry powder and flour and cook for 2 to 3 minutes. Gradually blend in the milk, bring to the boil, stirring, and simmer for 2 minutes. Stir in the fish, egg and salt and pepper to taste. Divide between the tartlet cases.
TO FREEZE: Place on a baking sheet and freeze uncovered, then remove tins and pack in a rigid container. Seal, label and return to the freezer.
TO SERVE: Unwrap, replace in the tins, cover with foil and cook from frozen in a preheated moderately hot oven, 190°C (375°F), Gas Mark 5, for 35 minutes. Garnish with fennel.
Serves 6

Salmon Fish Balls

500 g (1 lb)
  potatoes, cooked
150 g (5 oz) butter
1 x 205 g (7½ oz)
  can salmon,
  drained
1 tablespoon chopped
  parsley
salt and pepper
milk to bind
50 g (2 oz) fresh
  chives, chopped
1 egg, beaten
50 g (2 oz) fresh
  breadcrumbs
TO SERVE:
oil for deep frying
parsley sprigs

Cream the potatoes with 25 g (1 oz)
of the butter. Mix in the salmon,
parsley, and salt and pepper to taste
and bind with a little milk. Divide
the mixture into 6 and shape each
portion into a cake. Chill.

Beat the remaining butter until
softened then beat in the chives.
Spoon onto greaseproof paper. Chill.

When hard, divide into 6 and put a
portion on each fish cake. Shape the
cake into a ball round the butter and
roll in beaten egg and breadcrumbs.

TO FREEZE: Place on a tray and freeze
unwrapped until hard, then pack in a
polythene bag, seal, label and return
to the freezer.

TO SERVE: Place the fish balls on a
tray, cover loosely and thaw at room
temperature for about 3 hours, then
deep fry in the hot oil for about 10
minutes, until golden brown. Garnish
with parsley.
Serves 6

Cheesy Fish Pie

500 g (1 lb) cod fillet
1 bouquet garni
6 peppercorns
pinch of salt
1 tablespoon lemon
    juice
1 x 368 g (13 oz)
    packet frozen puff
    pastry, thawed
300 ml (½ pint)
    Béchamel Sauce
    (see page 16)
50 g (2 oz) Cheddar
    cheese, grated

Put the cod in a roasting pan with the bouquet garni, peppercorns, salt and lemon juice. Add water to cover and cook in a preheated moderate oven, 180°C (350°F), Gas Mark 4, for 15 minutes. Drain and cool.

Roll out the pastry to a large rectangle and place on a baking sheet.

Discard the skin and any bones from the fish, divide into pieces and stir into the Béchamel Sauce. Spoon this filling over one half of the pastry and sprinkle with the cheese. Fold the pastry, enclosing the filling, and press the edges together to seal.

TO FREEZE: Freeze uncovered on the baking sheet, then place on a piece of cardboard, cut to fit. Wrap in foil and place in a polythene bag. Seal, label and return to the freezer.

TO SERVE: Unwrap and place on the baking sheet. Cook from frozen in a preheated hot oven, 220°C (425°F), Gas Mark 7, for 30 minutes. Reduce the heat to moderate, 180°C (350°F), Gas Mark 4, and cook for a further 30 to 40 minutes until golden brown.

Serves 4

Smoked Haddock Flan

PASTRY:

250 g (8 oz) plain
  flour
pinch of salt
50 g (2 oz) lard
50 g (2 oz)
  margarine
3 tablespoons water
  (approximately)

FILLING:

250 g (8 oz) smoked
  haddock fillet
2 rashers streaky
  bacon, derinded
  and chopped
2 eggs
150 ml (¼ pint)
  milk
pepper
25 g (1 oz) Cheddar
  cheese, grated

TO SERVE:

parsley sprigs

Make the pastry and chill as for Curried Fish Tartlets (see page 24).

Roll out on a lightly floured surface and use to line a 20 to 23 cm (8 to 9 inch) freezerproof flan dish.

Put the haddock in a pan and cover with cold water. Bring to the boil and poach for about 10 minutes. Drain and cool, then discard any skin and bones. Flake the fish.

Fry the bacon gently in its own fat until crisp. Place the fish and bacon in the flan case. Whisk together the eggs and milk, pour into the flan and sprinkle with pepper and the cheese.

Place on a hot baking sheet and cook in a preheated moderately hot oven, 190°C (375°F), Gas Mark 5, for 25 to 30 minutes, until the filling is set. Cool.

TO FREEZE: Place in a polythene bag, seal, label and freeze.

TO SERVE: Unwrap and reheat from frozen in a preheated moderate oven, 180°C (350°F), Gas Mark 4, for 40 minutes or until heated through. Garnish with parsley.

Serves 4

Prawn Vol-au-Vents

*1 x 368 g (13 oz)
    packet frozen puff
    pastry, thawed*
*1 teaspoon anchovy
    essence*
*150 ml (¼ pint)
    Béchamel Sauce
    (see page 16)*
TO SERVE:
1 egg, beaten
*150 g (5 oz) frozen
    peeled prawns,
    thawed*

Roll out the pastry to a 5mm
(¼ inch) thickness and cut into
rounds, using a 3.5 cm (1½ inch)
pastry cutter. Use a 2.5 cm (1 inch)
cutter to mark circles in the centre of
each round, but do not cut right
through the pastry. Stir the anchovy
essence into the Béchamel Sauce.

TO FREEZE: Place the pastry cases on a
tray and freeze unwrapped, until
hard, then pack in a rigid container,
separating the layers. Pour the sauce
into a rigid container. Seal, label and
freeze both containers.

TO SERVE: Unwrap the pastry cases,
brush with beaten egg and place on a
baking sheet. Leave to stand at room
temperature for 30 minutes, then
cook in a preheated hot oven, 220°C
(425°F), Gas Mark 7, for 15 minutes,
until well risen and golden.

   Meanwhile, turn the sauce into a
saucepan and thaw over low heat.
Add the prawns and heat gently,
stirring, for about 10 minutes until
heated through.

   Remove the pastry lids from the
vol-au-vents. Spoon the sauce into
the pastry cases, replace the lids and
serve.

Makes 30 to 36

Braised Beef with Soured Cream

2 tablespoons oil
750 g (1½ lb) blade
  steak, cubed
1 onion, thinly sliced
250 g (8 oz)
  mushrooms, sliced
150 ml (¼ pint) beef
  stock
salt and pepper
TO SERVE:
142 ml (5 fl oz)
  fresh sour cream
1 teaspoon chopped
  parsley

Heat the oil in a frying pan and fry the meat, a few pieces at a time, until evenly browned, removing the pieces as they are browned. Add the onion and cook gently until soft. Return the meat to the pan, add the mushrooms, stock, and salt and pepper to taste and bring to the boil. Cover and cook in a preheated moderate oven, 160°C (325°F), Gas Mark 3, for 1½ hours. Cool.

TO FREEZE: Spoon into a rigid container, seal, label and freeze.

TO SERVE: Turn into a saucepan and heat gently until thawed, then bring to the boil, cover and simmer for 15 to 20 minutes. Remove from the heat, stir in the cream and heat through without boiling. Garnish with parsley.

Serves 4

Lasagne

125 g (4 oz) lasagne
1 teaspoon salt
1 tablespoon oil
Bolognese Sauce (see
   page 14)
600 ml (1 pint)
   Béchamel Sauce
   (see page 16)
125 g (4 oz)
   Gruyère cheese,
   grated
50 g (2 oz)
   Parmesan cheese,
   grated

Cook the lasagne in plenty of boiling water, with the salt and oil, until *al dente,* tender but firm to the bite. Drain well.

Grease a large shallow foil dish and place a layer of lasagne in the bottom. Spoon over half the Bolognese Sauce, then half the Béchamel Sauce, and sprinkle with half the grated Gruyère. Repeat the layers, then top with the remaining lasagne and sprinkle with the Parmesan cheese. Cool.

TO FREEZE: Cover, place in a polythene bag, seal, label and freeze.

TO SERVE: Unwrap and cook from frozen in a preheated moderately hot oven, 190°C (375°F), Gas Mark 5, for about 1 hour until heated through.

Serves 4

Beef Curry

1 teaspoon ground
  cinnamon
2 teaspoons paprika
1 1/2 teaspoons each
  ground turmeric,
  coriander, cumin,
  mustard, ginger
  and black pepper
1/2 teaspoon crushed
  chillis
1 tablespoon wine
  vinegar
1 1/2 teaspoons
  anchovy essence
6 tablespoons oil
3 onions, chopped
600 ml (1 pint) beef
  stock
1 x 227 g (8 oz) can
  tomatoes
2 cloves garlic, crushed
25 g (1 oz) dried
  apricots
1 bay leaf
750 g (1 1/2 lb) stewing
  steak, cubed
1 teaspoon salt

Place all the spices in a small bowl
and mix to a dryish paste with the
vinegar and anchovy essence.

Heat the oil in a pan, add the
onion and fry gently until soft. Stir
in the spice mixture and cook,
stirring, for 2 to 3 minutes.

Add the stock, tomatoes with their
juice, garlic, apricots and bay leaf.
Bring to the boil and simmer for
about 15 minutes. Add the beef and
salt, cover and simmer for about 2
hours. Cool.

TO FREEZE: Spoon into a foil dish.
Cover, place in a polythene bag, seal,
label and freeze.

TO SERVE: Turn into a saucepan and
thaw over gentle heat, then bring to
the boil. Cover and simmer for 30
minutes, adding a little water if the
curry becomes dry. Serve with
boiled rice, chutney and poppadoms.
Serves 4

Belgian Steak

3 tablespoons oil
2 large onions, sliced
125 g (4 oz)
    mushrooms,
    halved
750 g (1½ lb) blade
    or chuck steak, cut
    into 4 pieces
salt and pepper
2 tablespoons plain
    flour
300 ml (½ pint)
    lager
1 clove garlic crushed
1 tablespoon brown
    sugar
TO SERVE:
1 chicory leaf, sliced

Heat the oil in a pan, add the onions and fry until just coloured. Place in a casserole with the mushrooms.

Sprinkle the steaks with salt and pepper and coat with flour. Fry in the oil remaining in the pan until evenly browned then place in the casserole.

Sprinkle any leftover flour into the pan and blend into the fat; cook, stirring, until well browned, then remove from the heat and stir in the lager. Add the garlic, sugar and salt and pepper to taste and bring to the boil. Pour over the beef, cover and cook in a preheated moderate oven, 160°C (325°F), Gas Mark 3, for 2 hours. Cool.

TO FREEZE: Transfer to a foil dish. Cover, place in a polythene bag, seal, label and freeze.

TO SERVE: Uncover and reheat from frozen in a preheated moderately hot oven, 190°C (375°F), Gas Mark 5, for 1 hour. Cover with foil, lower the temperature to 160°C (325°F), Gas Mark 3, and cook for 45 minutes. Garnish with the chicory.

Serves 4

Swiss Beef

3 tablespoons oil
3 large onions, sliced
2 sticks celery, sliced
750 g (1½ lb) blade
  or chuck steak, cut
  into 4 pieces
salt and pepper
2 tablespoons plain
  flour
1 x 397 g (14 oz)
  can tomatoes
1 tablespoon tomato
  purée
1 clove garlic,
  crushed
TO SERVE:
chopped fresh basil

Heat the oil in a pan, add the onions and celery and fry gently until just coloured; transfer to a casserole.

Sprinkle the steaks with salt and pepper and coat with flour. Add to the pan and brown both sides, then place in the casserole.

Sprinkle any leftover flour into the pan and blend into the fat; cook, stirring, for 1 minute then add the remaining ingredients, with salt and pepper to taste. Bring to the boil and pour over the beef. Cover and cook in a preheated moderate oven, 160°C (325°F), Gas Mark 3, for 1½ to 2 hours. Cool.

TO FREEZE: Transfer to a foil dish. Cover, place in a polythene bag, seal, label and freeze.

TO SERVE: Reheat as for Belgian Steak (see page 33). Garnish with basil.
Serves 4

Chilli con Carne

500 g (1 lb) minced
  beef
1 large onion, chopped
½ green pepper,
  chopped
1 x 397 (14 oz) can
  tomatoes
2 tablespoons tomato
  purée
1 clove garlic, crushed
1 tablespoon chilli
  seasoning
¼ teaspoon cayenne
  pepper
salt and pepper
1 x 425 g (15 oz)
  can red kidney beans
TO SERVE:
1 tablespoon cornflour,
  blended with
  2 tablespoons water

Put the beef in a large saucepan and cook gently in its own fat, stirring, until evenly browned. Add the onion and green pepper and cook until soft.

Stir in the tomatoes with their juice, tomato purée, garlic, chilli seasoning, cayenne and salt and pepper to taste. Bring to the boil, cover and simmer for about 50 minutes, stirring occasionally. Stir in the kidney beans and cool.

TO FREEZE: Pour into a rigid container, cover, seal, label and freeze.

TO SERVE: Turn into a saucepan and heat gently until thawed, stirring occasionally, then bring to the boil, cover and simmer for 20 minutes, stirring occasionally. Stir in the cornflour and simmer, stirring, for 2 to 3 minutes. Serve with rice.
Serves 4

Steak and Kidney Pie

2 tablespoons oil
1 onion, sliced
750 g (1 ½ lb)
   stewing steak,
   cubed
225 g (8 oz) ox
   kidney, cubed
50 g (2 oz) plain
   flour
300 ml (½ pint) beef
   stock
1 teaspoon mixed
   herbs
salt and pepper
1 x 212 g (7½ oz)
   packet frozen puff
   pastry, thawed
TO SERVE:
1 egg, beaten

Heat the oil in a pan, add the onion and fry gently until soft. Coat the steak and kidney with flour, add to the pan and fry quickly until brown.

Gradually stir in the stock, herbs and salt and pepper to taste. Bring to the boil, cover and simmer for 1 to 1½ hours until the meat is just tender. Cool, then turn into a foil pie dish.

Roll out the pastry on a floured surface to a circle slightly larger than the dish and cut off a strip all round. Dampen the edge of the dish and place the strip on top. Moisten, then put the lid in position. Trim and seal the edges. Decorate with trimmings and cut a slit in the centre.

TO FREEZE: Wrap in plastic wrap, overwrap in foil, seal, label and freeze.
TO SERVE: Unwrap, brush with egg and cook from frozen in a preheated hot oven, 220°C (425°F), Gas Mark 7, for 30 minutes. Lower the heat to moderate, 180°C (350°F), Gas Mark 4, and bake for a further 30 minutes.
Serves 4 to 6

Stewed Lamb with Tomatoes

4 tablespoons oil
1.5 kg (3-3½ lb)
    middle neck of
    lamb
2 onions, sliced
1 x 397 g (14 oz)
    can tomatoes
1 x 65 g (2¼ oz)
    can tomato purée
600 ml (1 pint) stock
1 clove garlic,
    crushed
1 teaspoon each dried
    basil and
    marjoram
1 bay leaf
salt and pepper
TO SERVE:
1 tablespoon cornflour,
    blended with
    2 tablespoons water

Heat the oil in a pan and brown the lamb, a few pieces at a time, transferring the pieces to a large casserole as they brown. Add the onions to the pan and cook until soft. Stir in the remaining ingredients, with salt and pepper to taste. Bring to the boil, then pour over the lamb. Cover and cook in a preheated cool oven, 150°C (300°F), Gas Mark 2, for 3 hours.

Remove the lamb. Allow the sauce to cool, then skim off the fat. Cut the meat from the bones and place in a foil dish. Pour over the sauce.

TO FREEZE: Cover, place in a polythene bag, seal, label and freeze.

TO SERVE: Turn into a saucepan and thaw over very low heat, then bring to the boil. Cover and simmer, stirring occasionally, for 20 minutes. Stir in the blended cornflour and simmer, stirring, for 2 to 3 minutes until thickened. Check the seasoning. Serve with tagliatelle.

Serves 4

Spiced Lamb

2 tablespoons oil
750 g (1½ lb) boned
  leg of lamb, cubed
2 onions, chopped
8 tablespoons red wine
2 x 227 g (8 oz)
  cans tomatoes
2 cloves garlic, crushed
1 teaspoon turmeric
½ teaspoon each
  ground ginger and
  chilli seasoning
125 g (4 oz) seedless
  raisins
salt
TO SERVE:
50 g (2 oz) split
  blanched almonds,
  toasted

Heat the oil in a pan and brown the
meat, a few pieces at a time,
removing the pieces as they brown.
Add the onions to the pan and cook,
stirring, until soft. Return the meat
to the pan and add the remaining
ingredients, with salt to taste. Bring
to the boil, cover and simmer for
about 1½ hours. Cool.
TO FREEZE: Spoon into a foil dish,
cover, place in a polythene bag, seal,
label and freeze.
TO SERVE: Unwrap and reheat from
frozen in a preheated moderately hot
oven, 190°C (375°F), Gas Mark 5, for
1½ hours, or until heated through,
covering with foil when the meat is
thawed. Sprinkle with the almonds.
Serves 4

Wellington Lamb Cutlets

4 lamb cutlets
salt and pepper
2 tablespoons oil
125 g (4 oz) smooth
  liver pâté
1 x 212 g (7½ oz)
  packet frozen puff
  pastry, thawed
TO SERVE:
1 egg, beaten
tomato wedges
parsley sprigs

Sprinkle the cutlets with salt and
pepper. Heat the oil in a frying pan,
add the cutlets and fry quickly until
well browned. Let them cool, then
spread each one with a quarter of the
pâté. Roll out the pastry to a 30 cm
(12 inch) square and cut into 4
squares. Place a cutlet in the centre of
each piece. Fold the pastry to enclose
the filling and press the edges
together to seal.
TO FREEZE: Place on a baking sheet
and freeze uncovered until firm. Pack
in a rigid box, seal, label and return
to the freezer.
TO SERVE: Unwrap and place on a
baking sheet. Brush with beaten egg
and cut a slit in the top of each one.
Cook from frozen in a preheated hot
oven, 220°C (425°F), Gas Mark 7, for
35 to 40 minutes. Garnish with
tomato wedges and parsley.
Serves 4

Cassoulet

500 g (1 lb) dried
 haricot beans,
 soaked overnight
250 g (8 oz) streaky
 bacon, derinded
 and chopped
4 cloves garlic,
 crushed
2 tablespoons oil
500 g (1 lb) boned
 shoulder of lamb,
 cubed
2-3 chicken joints,
 halved
1 bouquet garni
450 ml (¾ pint)
 chicken stock
salt and pepper
125 g (4 oz) piece of
 French garlic
 sausage
1 x 397 g (14 oz)
 can tomatoes
1 tablespoon tomato
 purée
1 teaspoon sugar
50 g (2 oz) browned
 breadcrumbs

Drain the beans, cover with fresh water and place in a large pan. Bring to the boil, add the bacon and garlic and simmer for 1½ hours. Drain.

Heat the oil in a separate pan and fry the lamb and chicken until evenly browned. Add to the beans, with the bouquet garni, stock and plenty of black pepper. Cover and simmer for 2 hours. Add the sausage and cook for 1 hour or until the beans are tender, adding more stock if necessary.

Meanwhile, place the tomatoes with their juice, purée, sugar and a little salt and pepper in a pan. Bring to the boil, stirring, then simmer for 20 minutes or until thickened. Cool.

Transfer the bean mixture to a foil dish. Cool, slice the sausage and return to the mixture. Spoon the tomato pulp over the top. Sprinkle with the breadcrumbs.

TO FREEZE: Cover, place in a polythene bag, seal, label and freeze.
TO SERVE: Thaw overnight in the refrigerator, then uncover and reheat in a preheated moderately hot oven, 190°C (375°F), Gas Mark 5, for 30 to 40 minutes. Check the seasoning.
Serves 4 to 6

Summer Pork Casserole

50 g (2 oz) plain
    flour
salt and pepper
750 g (1½ lb) boned
    shoulder of pork,
    cubed
50 g (2 oz) butter
2 onions, sliced
2 celery sticks, sliced
1 red pepper, cored,
    seeded and chopped
2 courgettes, thickly
    sliced
225 g (8 oz)
    tomatoes, skinned,
    seeded and chopped
1 bouquet garni
1 tablespoon white
    wine vinegar
150 ml (¼ pint)
    tomato juice

Season the flour with salt and pepper and use to coat the pork. Melt the butter in a pan, add the pork and brown quickly. Transfer to a foil dish.

Add the onion, celery, red pepper and courgettes to the pan and cook gently until softened. Transfer to the casserole and add the tomatoes and bouquet garni. Add the vinegar, tomato juice, salt and pepper to taste.

Cover and cook in a preheated moderate oven, 180°C (350°F), Gas Mark 4, for about 1 hour, until just tender. Remove bouquet garni. Cool.

TO FREEZE: Cover, place in a polythene bag, seal, label and freeze.

TO SERVE: Remove the lid, cover with foil and reheat from frozen in a preheated moderate oven, 180°C (350°F), Gas Mark 4, for about 1 hour. Check the seasoning.

Serves 4

Spicy Pork Chops

1 teaspoon each dry
    mustard and
    ground ginger
1 tablespoon each
    Worcestershire
    sauce, vinegar,
    lemon juice and
    brown sugar
2 tablespoons tomato
    purée
salt and pepper
2 tablespoons
    dripping
4 pork chops
12 shallots or small
    onions
300 ml (½ pint)
    chicken stock
TO SERVE:
2 teaspoons cornflour,
    blended with
    1 tablespoon water

Mix together the mustard, ginger, sauce, vinegar, lemon juice, sugar, tomato purée and a little salt and pepper.

Heat the dripping in a frying pan and fry the chops, two at a time, until brown all over; transfer to a casserole. Fry the onions in the pan until browned; add to the casserole.

Pour off any remaining fat and add the stock and seasoning mixture to the pan. Bring to the boil, stirring. Pour over the chops, cover and cook in a preheated moderate oven, 180°C (350°F), Gas Mark 4, for 45 minutes.

TO FREEZE: Cool, transfer to a foil dish. Freeze as above.

TO SERVE: Reheat as above, stirring in the cornflour after 45 minutes.

Serves 4

Veal Chasseur

25 g (1 oz) butter
1 tablespoon oil
1 onion, chopped
1 green pepper,
    chopped
1 clove garlic, crushed
750 g (1½ lb)
    stewing veal,
    cubed
1 x 397 g (14 oz)
    can tomatoes,
    drained
25 g (1 oz) plain
    flour
150 ml (¼ pint) dry
    white wine
300 ml (½ pint)
    light stock
salt and pepper
225 g (8 oz)
    mushrooms, sliced
TO SERVE:
chopped parsley

Heat the butter and oil in a flameproof casserole. Add the onion, pepper and garlic and fry gently until soft. Add the veal and brown quickly all over. Add the tomatoes and cook, stirring, for a few minutes.

Stir in the flour and cook for 1 minute, then stir in the wine and stock. Bring to the boil, stirring, and add salt and pepper to taste.

Cover and cook in a preheated moderate oven, 180°C (350°F), Gas Mark 4, for 45 minutes. Add the mushrooms and cook for 15 minutes. Cool.

TO FREEZE: Turn into a rigid container, cover, label, seal and freeze.

TO SERVE: Turn into a saucepan and heat gently until thawed, stirring occasionally, then bring to the boil and simmer for 10 minutes. Check the seasoning. Sprinkle with parsley.
Serves 4

Pork and Pepper Casserole

2 tablespoons oil
1 onion, sliced
½ green pepper,
    sliced
½ red pepper, sliced
750 g (1½ lb)
    shoulder of pork,
    cubed
600 ml (1 pint) hot
    beef stock
2 teaspoons tomato
    purée
1 bay leaf
salt and pepper
TO SERVE:
1 tablespoon cornflour,
    blended with
    2 tablespoons water

Heat the oil in a pan, add the onion and peppers and fry gently until soft. Transfer to a casserole with a slotted spoon. Brown the pork in the pan, then add to the casserole with the remaining ingredients. Cover and cook in a preheated moderate oven, 160°C (325°F), Gas Mark 3, for 1½ hours. Cool.

TO FREEZE: Turn into a foil dish. Cover, place in a polythene bag, seal, label and freeze.

TO SERVE: Uncover and reheat from frozen in a preheated moderately hot oven, 190°C (375°F), Gas Mark 5, for 1 hour. Cover with foil and cook for a further 30 minutes. Stir in the blended cornflour and return to the oven, uncovered, for 10 minutes.
Serves 4

Almond Chicken Curry

1 tablespoon oil
2 onions, chopped
1 clove garlic,
 chopped
3 tablespoons curry
 powder
1 kg (2 lb) oven-
 ready chicken,
 jointed and skinned
2 teaspoons tomato
 purée
4 tablespoons lemon
 juice
300 ml (½ pint)
 chicken stock
1 bay leaf
TO SERVE:
25 g (1 oz) slivered
 almonds, toasted
salt

Heat the oil in a pan, add the onion and garlic and cook gently until soft. Stir in the curry powder and fry for 5 minutes, stirring. Add the chicken joints and fry until lightly browned on all sides, then add the tomato purée, lemon juice, bay leaf and stock. Bring to the boil, cover and simmer for about 1½ hours. Discard the bay leaf and cool.

TO FREEZE: Spoon into a foil dish. Cover, place in a polythene bag, seal, label and freeze.

TO SERVE: Uncover and reheat from frozen in a preheated moderate oven, 180°C (350°F), Gas Mark 4, for 2 hours, covering the dish when thawed to prevent it drying out. Sprinkle with the almonds and serve with rice.
Serves 4

Chicken Marengo

3 tablespoons oil
1 onion, chopped
1 carrot, chopped
2 sticks celery,
 chopped
25 g (1 oz) plain
 flour
450 ml (¾ pint)
 chicken stock
1 ½ tablespoons
 tomato purée
1 bouquet garni
4 chicken joints
½ x 227 g (8 oz)
 can tomatoes,
 drained
1 clove garlic,
 crushed
5 tablespoons dry
 vermouth
50 g (2 oz) button
 mushrooms
TO SERVE:
50 g (2 oz) frozen
 shelled prawns
8 cooked, unshelled
 prawns (optional)

Heat 2 tablespoons of the oil in a small saucepan. Add the onion, carrot and celery and cook until just beginning to colour. Stir in the flour and cook, stirring, until browned. Remove from the heat and gradually stir in the stock. Add half the tomato purée, and the bouquet garni. Bring to the boil, stirring, cover and simmer for about 30 minutes.

Meanwhile, heat the remaining oil in a large pan and brown the chicken joints on all sides; remove from the pan. Add the tomatoes, remaining purée and garlic to the pan and cook until pulped. Add the vermouth, mushrooms and chicken.

Discard the bouquet garni, skim the sauce and add to the chicken. Cover and simmer for 30 minutes. Cool.

TO FREEZE: Spoon into a foil dish. Cover, place in a polythene bag, seal, label and freeze.

TO SERVE: Unwrap and reheat from frozen in a preheated moderately hot oven, 200°C (400°F), Gas Mark 6, for 1 hour. Stir in the frozen prawns, cover with foil and return to the oven for 30 minutes. Garnish with whole prawns, if liked.
Serves 4

Individual Chicken Pies

25 g (1 oz) butter
25 g (1 oz) flour
300 ml (½ pint)
  chicken stock
grated rind of 1
  lemon
2 tablespoons lemon
  juice
2 tablespoons
  chopped parsley
500 g (1 lb) cooked
  chicken meat,
  chopped
salt and pepper
1 x 368 g (13 oz)
  packet frozen puff
  pastry, thawed
TO SERVE:
1 egg, beaten

Melt the butter in a pan, stir in the flour and cook, stirring, for 2 to 3 minutes. Gradually blend in the stock and cook, stirring, until thickened. Remove from the heat. Stir in the lemon rind and juice, parsley, chicken and salt and pepper to taste.

Roll out two thirds of the pastry thinly, cut out four 14 cm (5½ inch) circles and use to line four 10 cm (4 inch) foil dishes. Roll out the remaining pastry and cut out four circles for lids. Divide the chicken mixture between the pies, damp the edges of the pastry and cover with the lids. Trim and seal the edges. Chill.

TO FREEZE: Place on a baking sheet and open freeze. Wrap the pies individually in a double layer of foil. Seal, label and return to the freezer.

TO SERVE: Remove the foil, place the pies on a baking sheet and brush with beaten egg. Cook from frozen in a preheated hot oven, 220°C (425°F), Gas Mark 7, for about 30 minutes, until golden brown and heated through, cutting a slit in the top when the pastry is thawed.

Makes 4

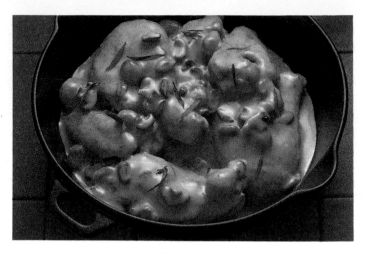

Suffolk Chicken

1 tablespoon oil
50 g (2 oz) butter
1.25 kg (3 lb) oven-
ready chicken, jointed
12 button onions or
shallots
2 tablespoons plain
flour
300 ml (½ pint)
light red wine
150 ml (¼ pint)
water
salt and pepper
1 bouquet garni
50 g (2 oz)
mushrooms, sliced
TO SERVE:
2 egg yolks
2 tablespoons cream
tarragon sprigs
(optional)

Heat the oil and butter in a large pan. Add the chicken joints and brown evenly, then remove. Add the onions to the pan and sauté until golden.

Stir in the flour and cook until just beginning to colour, then gradually blend in the wine and water. Add salt and pepper to taste and the bouquet garni. Bring to the boil. Add the mushrooms and chicken. Cover and simmer for 40 minutes. Discard the bouquet garni and cool. TO FREEZE: Place the chicken in a foil dish, surround with the vegetables, then pour over the sauce. Cover, place in a polythene bag, seal, label and freeze. TO SERVE: Thaw in wrappings in the refrigerator overnight. Unwrap, then cover loosely with fresh foil and place in a preheated moderately hot oven, 190°C (375°F), Gas Mark 5, for 1 hour. Transfer the chicken and vegetables to a serving dish. Keep hot.

Beat the egg yolks and cream together and stir in a little of the sauce. Stir slowly into the sauce then return to the oven for 1 to 2 minutes to heat through. Pour over the chicken and garnish with tarragon, if liked.
Serves 4 to 6

Chicken Suprême with Mushrooms

65 g (2½ oz) butter
2 onions, finely
  chopped
125 g (4 oz)
  mushrooms,
  chopped
salt and pepper
4 tablespoons dry
  white wine
1 teaspoon tomato
  purée
4 tablespoons chicken
  stock
4 boned chicken
  breasts
TO SERVE:
1 tablespoon chopped
  parsley

Melt 15 g (½ oz) of the butter in a pan. Add the onions and sauté until soft. Add the mushrooms and salt and pepper to taste and cook until soft.

Add the wine, tomato purée and stock and continue cooking, stirring, until the liquid is well concentrated; chill.

Beat out the chicken breasts to an even thickness and place each one on a sheet of foil. Divide the mushroom mixture between them and dot with the remaining butter. Fold the foil over the top and seal the edges.

TO FREEZE: Place on a baking sheet and open freeze, then pack in a polythene bag. Seal, label and return to the freezer.

TO SERVE: Place the foil parcels on a baking sheet. Cook from frozen in a preheated hot oven, 220°C (425°F), Gas Mark 7, for about 1 hour. Remove the foil and sprinkle with parsley.

Serves 4

Turkey Blanquette

750 g (1½ lb)
  cooked turkey
  meat, sliced
25 g (1 oz) butter
25 g (1 oz) plain
  flour
300 ml (½ pint)
  turkey or chicken
  stock
TO SERVE:
1 egg yolk
2 tablespoons cream
chopped parsley

Arrange the turkey in a foil pie dish.
Melt the butter in a small pan and
stir in the flour. Cook, stirring, for 1
to 2 minutes. Remove from the heat
and gradually stir in the stock.
Return to the heat and cook, stirring,
for 1 to 2 minutes; cool.

TO FREEZE: Spoon the sauce over the
turkey. Cover, place in a polythene
bag, seal, label and freeze.

TO SERVE: Cover the dish loosely
with foil and reheat from frozen in a
preheated moderately hot oven,
190°C (375°F), Gas Mark 5, for 1 hour.

Beat the egg yolk and cream
together and add a little of the hot
sauce; blend well then mix into the
sauce in the dish. Return to the oven
for 3 minutes. Garnish with parsley.
Serves 4

Stuffed Turkey Roll

750 g-1 kg
  (1½-2 lb) boned
  turkey breast
2 tablespoons oil
1 large onion,
  chopped
25 g (1 oz) seedless
  raisins
15 g (½ oz)
  blanched almonds,
  split
25 g (1 oz) dried
  apricots, chopped
½ tablespoon
  chopped parsley
1 tablespoon lemon
  juice
salt and pepper

Beat the turkey breast to flatten.

Heat half the oil in a pan, add the
onion and cook until soft. Add the
raisins and almonds and cook for 1
to 2 minutes, stirring. Stir in the
remaining ingredients.

Spoon the stuffing mixture along
the centre of the turkey and roll up.
Secure with cocktail sticks and tie
with fine string.

Brush with the remaining oil and
sprinkle with salt and pepper. Roast
in a preheated moderate oven, 160°C
(325°F), Gas Mark 3, for about 1½
hours. Cool.

TO FREEZE: Remove the cocktail sticks
and string. Wrap the roll tightly in
foil or plastic wrap. Place in a
polythene bag, seal, label and freeze.

TO SERVE: Thaw in wrappings in the
refrigerator for 24 hours. Serve
sliced, with salad.
Serves 4 to 6

Duck with Olives

2 tablespoons oil
2 kg (4½ lb)
  duckling,
  quartered
1 onion, sliced
1 teaspoon paprika
90 ml (3 fl oz) sweet
  sherry
300 ml (½ pint) beef
  stock
1 bouquet garni
1 x 227 g (8 oz) can
  tomatoes
TO SERVE:
2 teaspoons cornflour,
  blended with
  1 tablespoon water
50 g (2 oz) large
  black olives

Heat the oil in a flameproof casserole and brown the duckling evenly, two pieces at a time. Remove and pour off most of the fat, then add the onion and cook until soft. Stir in the paprika and cook for 1 to 2 minutes.

Return the duck to the casserole. Warm the sherry, pour over the duck and ignite. When the flames die, add the stock, bouquet garni and tomatoes with their juice. Bring to the boil, cover and cook in a preheated moderate oven, 180°C (350°F), Gas Mark 4, for 45 minutes. Cool.

TO FREEZE: Arrange in a foil dish. Cover, place in a polythene bag, seal, label and freeze.

TO SERVE: Thaw in wrappings in the refrigerator overnight. Unwrap, cover loosely with fresh foil and reheat in a preheated moderately hot oven, 190°C (375°F), Gas Mark 5, for 40 minutes. Stir in the blended cornflour, add the olives and return to the oven, uncovered, for 15 minutes.
Serves 4

Pigeons en Cocotte

2 tablespoons oil
4 pigeons
125 g (4 oz) streaky
  bacon, derinded
  and chopped
12 button onions
125 g (4 oz) button
  mushrooms, halved
5 tablespoons dry
  vermouth
200 ml (⅓ pint)
  chicken stock
salt and pepper
TO SERVE:
1 tablespoon cornflour,
  blended with
  2 tablespoons water

Heat the oil in a large frying pan and brown the pigeons evenly, two at a time; transfer to a casserole. Add the bacon and onions to the pan and cook until just beginning to brown.

Add the remaining ingredients, with salt and pepper to taste. Bring to the boil and pour over the pigeons. Cover and cook in a preheated moderate oven, 160°C (325°F), Gas Mark 3, for 1½ hours. Cool.

TO FREEZE: Freeze as above.

TO SERVE: Thaw, reheat and thicken with cornflour as above.
Serves 4

Poachers' Pie

2 tablespoons oil
2 pigeons
½ rabbit, jointed
500 g (1 lb) shin of
    beef, cubed
1.2 litres (2 pints)
    beef stock
salt and pepper
125 g (4 oz)
    mushrooms,
    halved
2 tablespoons
    cornflour, blended
    with 4 tablespoons
    water
1 x 368 g (13 oz)
    packet frozen puff
    pastry, thawed
TO SERVE:
1 egg yolk, beaten

Heat the oil in a large frying pan and brown the pigeons, rabbit and beef evenly, a few pieces at a time. Return to the pan and add the stock and salt and pepper to taste. Bring to the boil, cover and simmer for 2 hours.

Add the mushrooms and simmer for 30 minutes. Strain and reserve 600 ml (1 pint) of the stock. Cut the meat from the pigeons and rabbit. Place all the meat and mushrooms in a foil pie dish; chill.

Stir the blended cornflour into the stock and heat gently, stirring, until thickened. Cool, then pour into the pie dish. Roll out the pastry thinly and use to cover the pie; chill.

TO FREEZE: Open freeze, then put into a polythene bag. Seal, label and return to the freezer.

TO SERVE: Unwrap, place on a baking sheet and brush with egg yolk. Cook from frozen in a preheated hot oven, 220°C (425°F), Gas Mark 7, for 30 minutes, cutting a slit in the top when the pastry is thawed. Reduce the heat to moderate, 180°C (350°F), Gas Mark 4, and bake for 30 minutes.
Serves 6

51

Aubergines au Gratin

3 large aubergines,
  sliced
salt and pepper
600 ml (1 pint)
  Tomato and
  Pepper Sauce (see
  page 12)
50 g (2 oz) Gruyère
  cheese, grated
1 tablespoon grated
  Parmesan cheese

Place the aubergines in a colander, sprinkle with salt and leave for 30 minutes. Drain, rinse and dry on kitchen paper. Blanch in boiling salted water for 1 minute, drain well and cool.

Layer the aubergines and sauce in a foil dish, sprinkle with salt and pepper to taste and top with the cheeses.

TO FREEZE: Cover, place in a polythene bag, seal, label and freeze.

TO SERVE: Uncover and cook from frozen in a preheated moderately hot oven, 190°C (375°F), Gas Mark 5, for 30 minutes, then lower the heat to 160°C (325°F), Gas Mark 3, and cook for a further 45 minutes or until cooked through.

Serves 4 to 6

Pommes Duchesse

1 kg (2 lb) potatoes
salt and pepper
50 g (2 oz) butter
1 egg, beaten
TO SERVE:
1 small egg, beaten
parsley sprigs

Simmer the potatoes in boiling salted water until tender, then drain and mash. Add the butter and beat until smooth. Beat in the egg and season well with salt and pepper. Cool.

TO FREEZE: Pipe in small whirls on a baking sheet and open freeze until hard. Pack in a rigid container, seal, label and return to the freezer.

TO SERVE: Place the whirls on baking sheets and thaw at room temperature for about 1 hour. Brush with beaten egg and reheat in a preheated moderately hot oven, 200°C (400°F), Gas Mark 6, for about 30 minutes, until browned. Garnish with parsley.

Serves 4 to 6

Vegetable Pie

1 kg (2 lb) potatoes, cooked
50 g (2 oz) butter
150 ml (¼ pint) milk
250 g (8 oz) shelled broad beans
2 carrots, diced
½ green pepper, sliced
2 small onions, chopped
½ small cauliflower, broken into florets
salt and pepper
4 small tomatoes, skinned and chopped
SAUCE:
15 g (½ oz) butter
15 g (½ oz) flour
150 ml (¼ pint) milk
½ teaspoon made mustard
25 g (1 oz) Cheddar cheese, grated

Cream the potatoes with the butter and milk. Place the remaining vegetables, except the tomatoes, in a pan of boiling salted water. Return to the boil, cover and simmer for 15 to 20 minutes; drain.

Meanwhile, put the tomatoes in a small pan with salt and pepper to taste and simmer gently until pulped. Spoon the mixed vegetables into a foil pie dish and season well with salt and pepper. Spoon over the tomato pulp.

To make the sauce, melt the butter in a small pan, stir in the flour and cook for 1 minute. Gradually stir in the milk and cook for 2 to 3 minutes, stirring. Add salt and pepper to taste, the mustard and cheese. Spoon the sauce over the vegetables and cover with the potatoes. Cool.

TO FREEZE: Cover, place in a polythene bag, seal, label and freeze.
TO SERVE: Uncover and reheat from frozen in a preheated moderately hot oven, 190°C (375°F), Gas Mark 5, for 45 minutes or until heated through and browned on top.
Serves 4

Chicory and Ham au Gratin

8 even-sized heads of chicory
2 teaspoons salt
8 slices cooked ham
125 g (4 oz) Cheddar cheese, grated
600 ml (1 pint) Béchamel Sauce (see page 16)
1 tablespoon fresh white breadcrumbs
TO SERVE:
parsley sprig

Cook the chicory in boiling salted water for 15 minutes. Drain and rinse in cold water, drain again. Wrap each piece of chicory in a slice of ham. Stir the cheese into the sauce.
TO FREEZE: Place the chicory in a foil dish. Spoon over the prepared sauce and sprinkle with the breadcrumbs. Cover, place in a polythene bag, seal, label and freeze.
TO SERVE: Unwrap and reheat from frozen as for Vegetable Pie (see above). Garnish with parsley.
Serves 4

Stuffed Onions

8 large onions
2 teaspoons salt
STUFFING:
2 tablespoons oil
250 g (8 oz) sausage
  meat
50 g (2 oz) fresh
  breadcrumbs
2 tablespoons
  chopped parsley
2 teaspoons dried
  thyme
salt and pepper
TO SERVE:
Tomato and Pepper
Sauce (see page 12)

Skin the onions but leave whole, with the roots intact. Cook in boiling salted water for 10 to 15 minutes until tender. Drain.

Heat the oil in a frying pan, add the sausage meat and fry gently for 10 minutes, breaking it up. Stir in the breadcrumbs, herbs, and salt and pepper to taste.

Trim the root end off each onion and push out the centres with your thumb. Chop the centres and add to the stuffing.

TO FREEZE: Pack the onions side by side in a foil dish and spoon the stuffing into the centres. Cool, cover, place in a polythene bag, seal, label and freeze.

TO SERVE: Unwrap then cover loosely with fresh foil. Bake from frozen in a preheated moderate oven, 180°C (350°F), Gas Mark 4, for 30 minutes. Serve with Tomato and Pepper Sauce.
Serves 4

Courgettes à la Grecque

*300 ml (½ pint) dry
  white wine*
juice of 2 lemons
*150 ml (¼ pint)
  water*
*5 tablespoons olive
  oil*
*1 thyme sprig
  (optional)*
1 parsley sprig
1 bay leaf
*½ teaspoon ground
  coriander*
salt and pepper
*500 g (1 lb)
  courgettes, thickly
  sliced*
TO SERVE:
*1 tablespoon chopped
  fennel (optional)*

Put the wine, lemon juice, water, oil, herbs, coriander and a little salt and pepper in a saucepan and bring to the boil. Put the courgettes in a blanching basket and immerse in the boiling liquid. Bring the liquid back to the boil and boil rapidly for 1 minute, then remove and drain the courgettes. Simmer the remaining liquid until it is well reduced. Cool.
TO FREEZE: Put the courgettes in a foil dish and pour the liquid over them. Cover, place in a polythene bag, seal, label and freeze.
TO SERVE: Thaw, covered, at room temperature for 2 to 3 hours. Serve cold, sprinkled with fennel, if liked.
Serves 4

Risotto

50 g (2 oz) streaky
   bacon, derinded
   and chopped
1 onion, chopped
1 celery stick,
   chopped
½ green pepper,
   chopped
½ red pepper,
   chopped
25 g (1 oz) butter
250 g (8 oz)
   long-grain rice
375 g (12 oz) cooked
   chicken, chopped
600 ml (1 pint)
   chicken stock
TO SERVE:
15 g (½ oz) butter
salt and pepper
1 tablespoon chopped
   thyme or parsley
2 tablespoons grated
   Parmesan cheese

Fry the bacon in a pan very gently until the fat runs, then add the onion, celery and peppers and fry gently until soft. Drain on kitchen paper.

Melt the butter in the same pan and add the rice. Fry for 2 to 3 minutes, stirring, until the fat is absorbed, then stir in the bacon, vegetables, chicken and stock. Bring to the boil, cover and simmer for 20 minutes or until the rice is tender and the liquid absorbed. Cool.

TO FREEZE: Spoon into a foil dish, cover, place in a polythene bag, seal, label and freeze.

TO SERVE: Uncover and flake the butter over the rice. Cover loosely with fresh foil and reheat from frozen in a preheated moderately hot oven, 190°C (375°F), Gas Mark 5, for about 1 hour, forking the rice over from time to time. Add salt and pepper to taste and stir in the herbs. Serve sprinkled with Parmesan.
Serves 4

Ratatouille

1 augerbine, sliced
salt and pepper
4 tablespoons olive
   oil
2 onions, sliced
3 courgettes, sliced
4 large, ripe
   tomatoes, skinned
   and sliced
1 clove garlic,
   crushed
1 bay leaf

Put the aubergine slices in a colander
sprinkle liberally with salt and leave
for 30 minutes, then drain, rinse and
dry on kitchen paper.

Heat the oil in a large pan, add the
onions and cook gently until soft.
Stir in the remaining ingredients,
with salt and pepper to taste. Cover
and simmer for about 30 minutes
until the vegetables are tender. Cool.
TO FREEZE: Spoon into a rigid
container. Cover, place in a
polythene bag, seal, label and freeze.
TO SERVE: If serving hot, turn into a
saucepan and thaw over a very low
heat, stirring occasionally, then bring
to the boil and simmer for 5 minutes.

If serving cold, uncover and thaw
at room temperature for 5 hours.

Check the seasoning before
serving.
Serves 4

Braised Red Cabbage

1 red cabbage,
  shredded
50 g (2 oz) butter
1 large onion, sliced
1 large cooking
  apple, sliced
1 tablespoon sugar
2 tablespoons wine
  vinegar
salt and pepper

Blanch the cabbage in a large pan of boiling water for about 5 minutes, then drain.

Melt half the butter in a pan, add the onion and apple and cook for about 5 minutes, until soft.

Spread about one third of the cabbage in a well greased ovenproof dish. Cover with one third of the onion and apple and sprinkle with a little sugar, vinegar, salt and pepper. Repeat the layers twice more.

Dot the remaining butter on top, cover with greaseproof paper, then with a lid or foil. Bake in a preheated moderate oven, 160°C (325°F), Gas Mark 3, for about 2 hours, stirring from time to time. Cool.

TO FREEZE: Spoon into a foil dish, cover, place in a polythene bag, seal, label and freeze.

TO SERVE: Thaw, covered, at room temperature for 3 to 4 hours, then unwrap and reheat in a preheated moderate oven, 160°C (325°F), Gas Mark 3, for about 30 minutes.
Serves 6

Chicken Liver Pâté

50 g (2 oz) butter
500 g (1 lb) chicken
  livers
1 onion, chopped
1 clove garlic,
  crushed
1 tablespoon cream
2 tablespoons tomato
  purée
3 tablespoons dry
  sherry
salt and pepper
TO SERVE:
parsley sprigs

Melt the butter in a frying pan. Add the chicken livers and fry for 2 to 3 minutes until lightly browned. Add the onion and garlic, cover and cook gently for about 5 minutes.

Stir in the cream, tomato purée and sherry and cool slightly, then purée in an electric blender or rub through a sieve. Add salt and pepper to taste.

TO FREEZE: Spoon into individual freezerproof ramekin dishes and smooth the tops. Cover each one, place them all in a polythene bag, seal, label and freeze.

TO SERVE: Thaw at room temperature for 3 hours. Garnish with parsley. Serve with toast or salad.

Serves 4

Meatballs with Pepper Dip

250 g (8 oz) minced
 beef
½ small onion,
 finely chopped
1 small egg, beaten
salt and pepper
oil for shallow frying
TO SERVE:
150 ml (¼ pint)
 fresh sour cream
½ small green
 pepper, finely
 chopped
½ small red pepper,
 finely chopped
1 clove garlic,
 crushed
pinch of chilli
 seasoning

Mix the meat and onion together and season well with salt and pepper. Bind with the egg. Shape into small balls, using floured hands.

Heat the oil in a frying pan and fry the meatballs, a few at a time, until well browned all over. Drain on kitchen paper and cool.

TO FREEZE: Pack in a single layer in a foil dish. Cover, place in a polythene bag, seal, label and freeze.

TO SERVE: Uncover and reheat from frozen in a preheated moderately hot oven, 200°C (400°F), Gas Mark 6, for 35 to 40 minutes, until piping hot.

Meanwhile, mix the sour cream with the chopped peppers, garlic, chilli seasoning and salt and pepper to taste in a dish. Serve the meatballs on cocktail sticks, with the dip.

Serves 4

Savoury Ham Puffs

CHOUX PASTRY:
150 ml (¼ pint)
   water
50 g (2 oz) butter
65 g (2½ oz) plain
   flour, sifted
2 eggs, beaten
50 g (2 oz)
   Parmesan cheese,
   grated
salt and pepper
FILLING:
25 g (1 oz) butter
1 onion, chopped
50 g (2 oz)
   mushrooms,
   chopped
1 tablespoon plain
   flour
150 ml (¼ pint)
   ham or chicken
   stock
1 tomato, skinned
   and chopped
125 g (4 oz) cooked
   ham, chopped
TO SERVE:
parsley sprigs

Put the water and butter in a saucepan and bring to the boil. Remove from the heat and quickly beat in the flour. Continue beating until the mixture forms a ball. Cool slightly, then gradually beat in the eggs, until smooth. Stir in the cheese and a little salt and pepper.

Divide between six 7.5 cm (3 inch) foil dishes and bake in a preheated moderately hot oven, 200°C (400°F), Gas Mark 6, for 15 to 20 minutes, until well risen and golden. Cool.

Meanwhile, prepare the filling. Melt the butter in a pan, add the onion and cook until soft. Add the mushrooms and cook for 1 to 2 minutes, then stir in the flour and cook for 1 minute. Blend in the stock. Simmer, stirring, for 5 minutes. Add tomato and ham; cool.

TO FREEZE: Pack the puffs in dishes in a box. Spoon filling into a separate container. Seal, label and freeze both.

TO SERVE: Unwrap the puffs and thaw at room temperature for about 2 hours. Spoon in the filling and bake in a preheated moderately hot oven, 200°C (400°F), Gas Mark 6, for about 15 minutes. Garnish with parsley.

Serves 6

Chicken Liver Vol–au–Vents

1 x 368 g (13 oz)
  packet frozen puff
  pastry, thawed
1 egg, beaten
FILLING:
25 g (1 oz) butter
250 g (8 oz) chicken
  livers, chopped
1 onion, chopped
2 mushrooms,
  chopped
1 tablespoon plain
  flour
150 ml (¼ pint)
  chicken stock
TO SERVE:
1 tablespoon grated
  Parmesan cheese
chopped parsley

Prepare the vol–au–vent cases as for
Prawn Vol–au–Vents (see page 29).

Melt the butter in a pan and fry
the chicken livers gently for 3 to 4
minutes, until lightly browned;
remove.

Add the onion to the pan and cook
until soft. Add the mushrooms and
cook for 1 to 2 minutes. Stir in the
flour, then stir in the stock. Simmer,
stirring, for about 5 minutes.
Remove from the heat, stir in the
livers and cool.

TO FREEZE: Freeze the pastry cases as
for Prawn Vol–au–Vents. Spoon the
filling into a rigid container. Seal,
label and freeze.

TO SERVE: Thaw the filling at room
temperature for 1½ hours. Thaw and
cook the pastry cases as for Prawn
Vol–au–Vents. Turn the filling into a
saucepan and heat gently, stirring,
for about 10 minutes, until heated
through. Remove the lids and spoon
the filling into the pastry cases.
Sprinkle with cheese and parsley and
replace the lids.
Makes 30 to 36

Mushroom and Pepper Pizzas

PIZZA BASE:
150 ml (¼ pint)
 milk
125 g (4 oz) butter
25 g (1 oz) fresh
 yeast
3 eggs, beaten
500 g (1 lb) plain
 flour
1 teaspoon salt

PIZZA TOPPING:
2 tablespoons oil
2 large onions,
 chopped
2 x 397 g (14 oz)
 cans tomatoes
2 cloves garlic,
 crushed
1 small bay leaf
1 teaspoon dried basil
1 teaspoon dried
 oregano
salt and pepper

TO FINISH:
125 g (4 oz)
 mushrooms, sliced
 and sautéed in
 butter
1 green pepper, sliced

Put the milk and butter in a small pan and heat gently until warm. Remove from the heat, add the yeast and blend well, then beat in the eggs.

Sift the flour and salt into a large bowl, add the yeast liquid and mix to a soft dough. Cover and leave to rise in a warm place for about 45 minutes.

Meanwhile, make the topping. Heat the oil in a frying pan, add the onions and cook gently until soft. Add the tomatoes with their juice, garlic, herbs and salt and pepper to taste and bring to the boil. Cook for about 20 minutes, stirring occasionally, until the sauce is thick. Cool.

Turn the dough onto a floured board and cut into 4 pieces. Roll each piece out to a 20 cm (8 inch) circle and place on a greased baking sheet. Stand a 20 cm (8 inch) flan ring round each one.

Divide the topping between the pizzas, and arrange the mushrooms and pepper slices on top. Cover and leave in a warm place for about 10 minutes.

TO FREEZE: Open freeze on the baking sheets, then remove the flan rings and wrap each pizza in foil or plastic wrap. Place each one in a polythene bag. Seal, label and return to the freezer.

TO SERVE: Unwrap, place on baking sheets and bake in a preheated hot oven, 230°C (450°F), Gas Mark 8, for 35 to 40 minutes until golden and firm. Serve with a crisp green salad.
Makes 4

Ham Pizzas

4 pizza bases
1 recipe pizza
   topping
TO FINISH:
125 g (4 oz) cooked
   ham, chopped
50 g (2 oz) large
   black olives

Place the pizzas on baking sheets and surround with flan rings, (see opposite). Mix the ham and olives into the topping and spoon over the pizzas.
   Rise, freeze, bake and serve as opposite.
Makes 4

Anchovy Pizzas

4 pizza bases
1 recipe pizza
   topping
TO FINISH:
250 g (8 oz)
   Cheddar cheese,
   sliced
2 x 50 g (1³/4 oz)
   cans anchovy
   fillets

Place the pizzas on baking sheets and surround with flan rings (see opposite). Spoon the topping over the pizzas, cover with cheese and arrange the anchovies on top.
   Rise, freeze, bake and serve as opposite.
Makes 4

65

Savoury Beef Pancakes

*250 g (8 oz) minced
    beef*
½ onion, chopped
1 carrot, chopped
*1 celery stick,
    chopped*
*150 ml (¼ pint) beef
    stock*
2 tablespoons sherry
*1 tablespoon tomato
    purée*
salt and pepper
*1 tablespoon cornflour,
    blended with
    2 tablespoons water*
*4 cooked pancakes
    (see page 76)*
TO SERVE:
*parsley sprigs
tomato*

Fry the beef in a dry frying pan,
stirring, until evenly browned. Add
the vegetables and cook, stirring,
until they are tender. Add the stock,
sherry, tomato purée, and salt and
pepper to taste. Cover and simmer
for about 45 minutes.

Stir in the blended cornflour.
Bring to the boil, stirring, and cook
for 1 to 2 minutes. Check the
seasoning. Cool, then divide between
the pancakes and roll up.

TO FREEZE: Place the pancakes in a
foil dish in a single layer. Cover,
place in a polythene bag, seal, label
and freeze.

TO SERVE: Uncover and reheat from
frozen in a preheated moderately hot
oven, 190°C (375°F), Gas Mark 5, for
45 to 50 minutes. Serve garnished
with parsley and sliced tomato.
Serves 4

Chicken and Mushroom Pancakes

50 g (2 oz) butter
½ onion, chopped
50 g (2 oz)
    mushrooms,
    chopped
2 tablespoons plain
    flour
300 ml (½ pint)
    milk
salt and pepper
100 g (4 oz) cooked
    chicken meat,
    chopped
25 g (1 oz) cooked
    ham, chopped
4 cooked pancakes
    (see page 76)
TO SERVE:
lettuce
tomatoes

Melt the butter in a pan, add the onion and mushrooms and cook gently for about 5 minutes until soft. Stir in the flour and cook for 1 minute, stirring. Remove from the heat and gradually stir in the milk. Season well with salt and pepper, then cool.

Stir the chicken and ham into the sauce. Divide between the pancakes and roll up.

Freeze and reheat as for Savoury Beef Pancakes (see opposite). Garnish with lettuce and tomato.
Serves 4

Mushroom Quiche

1 x 212 g (7½ oz)
   packet frozen
   shortcrust pastry,
   thawed
50 g (2 oz) butter
500 g (1 lb)
   mushrooms, sliced
1 large onion,
   chopped
squeeze of lemon
   juice
salt and pepper
1 tablespoon plain
   flour
150 ml (¼ pint)
   double cream
1 egg, beaten

Roll out the pastry and use to line a 23 cm (9 inch) foil flan dish. Prick well with a fork. Line with greaseproof paper and beans. Bake blind in a preheated hot oven, 230°C (450°F), Gas Mark 8, for 10 minutes. Remove the beans and paper. Cool.

Melt the butter in a saucepan, and cook the mushrooms and onion gently until soft. Add the lemon juice and salt and pepper to taste. Sprinkle in the flour and cook, stirring, for 2 minutes. Cool. Beat the cream into the egg, then stir into the filling. Pour into the flan case.

TO FREEZE: Open freeze, then cover and place in a polythene bag. Seal, label and return to the freezer.

TO SERVE: Unwrap and bake from frozen in a hot oven, 230°C (450°F), Gas Mark 8, for 10 minutes, then lower the heat to moderately hot, 190°C (375°F), Gas Mark 5, and bake for 20 to 30 minutes, until set.
Serves 6

Stuffed Peppers

25 g (1 oz) butter
125 g (4 oz) bacon,
   derinded and
   chopped
1 onion, chopped
125 g (4 oz) long-
   grain rice, cooked
50 g (2 oz)
   mushrooms, sliced
3 tomatoes, skinned
   and chopped
2 teaspoons chopped
   parsley
1 clove garlic, crushed
salt and pepper
4 green peppers
50 g (2 oz) Cheddar
   cheese, grated

Melt the butter in a pan, add the bacon and onion and fry until the bacon is crisp. Stir in the rice, mushrooms, tomatoes, parsley, garlic and salt and pepper to taste.

Cut the peppers in half and remove the seeds and pith. Blanch in boiling water for 3 minutes, drain and place in foil dishes. Fill with the rice mixture and sprinkle with cheese.

TO FREEZE: Cover, place in a polythene bag, seal, label and freeze.

TO SERVE: Unwrap, cover with foil and cook from frozen in a preheated hot oven, 220°C (425°F), Gas Mark 7, for 1 hour. Uncover and cook for 20 minutes until brown on top.
Serves 4

Cheese and Ham Croquettes

250 g (8 oz)
    potatoes, cooked
125 g (4 oz) ham,
    diced
125 g (4 oz)
    Cheddar cheese,
    grated
1 egg, beaten
¼ teaspoon cayenne
    pepper
2 teaspoons chopped
    parsley
salt and pepper
COATING:
1 egg, beaten
2 tablespoons milk
125 g (4 oz) dried
    white breadcrumbs
TO SERVE:
oil for deep frying
Tomato and Pepper
    Sauce (see page 12)

Mash the potatoes and mix with the ham, cheese, egg, cayenne and parsley. Add salt and pepper to taste and mix thoroughly. Divide equally into 8 pieces and roll each one into a sausage shape.

Beat the egg and milk together. Dip the croquettes into the egg mixture, then roll in the breadcrumbs to coat completely.

TO FREEZE: Open freeze on a baking sheet. Place in a polythene bag, seal, label and return to the freezer.

TO SERVE: Thaw, wrapped, in the refrigerator for 2 hours. Deep fry in the hot oil for 5 minutes or until golden. Drain on kitchen paper. Serve hot with Tomato and Pepper Sauce and a green salad.

Serves 4

Corinthian Coffee Cake

175 g (6 oz) butter
175 g (6 oz) caster
   sugar
3 eggs, beaten
175 g (6 oz)
   self-raising flour,
   sifted
TO SERVE:
300 ml (½ pint)
   strong black coffee,
   sweetened
4 tablespoons brandy
300 ml (½ pint)
   double cream,
   whipped
fruit or nuts to
   decorate

Cream the butter and sugar until light. Gradually beat in the eggs, then fold in the flour. Turn into a greased and floured 23 cm (9 inch) ring tin and bake in a preheated moderately hot oven, 190°C (375°F), Gas Mark 5, for about 25 minutes, until well risen. Cool on a wire rack.

TO FREEZE: Wrap in polythene, seal, label and freeze.

TO SERVE: Thaw at room temperature for about 1 hour, then unwrap and place on a serving dish.

Mix the coffee and brandy together and spoon over the cake. Cover with whipped cream and decorate with fruit or nuts.

Serves 4 to 6

Plum Crumb Pudding

1 kg (2 lb) plums,
  stoned
25 g (1 oz) sugar
300 ml (½ pint)
  water
175 g (6 oz)
  wholemeal
  breadcrumbs
50 g (2 oz) demerara
  sugar
50 g (2 oz) butter
TO SERVE:
150 ml (¼ pint)
  double cream,
  whipped
15 g (½ oz) flaked
  almonds (optional)

Place the plums, sugar and water in a saucepan and cook until soft; cool. Mix the breadcrumbs and sugar together. Melt the butter in a pan, add the crumb mixture and fry until crisp; cool. Layer the plums and crumbs alternately in a foil dish.

TO FREEZE: Cover, place in a polythene bag, seal, label and freeze.

TO SERVE: Uncover and reheat from frozen in a preheated moderately hot oven, 190°C (375°F), Gas Mark 5, for 30 minutes. Cover the top thickly with whipped cream and decorate with almonds, if liked.

Serves 6

Strawberry Ice Cream

1 kg (2 lb)
    strawberries
150 ml (¼ pint)
    water
150 g (5 oz) caster
    sugar
3 egg yolks, beaten
450 ml (¾ pint)
    whipping cream,
    lightly whipped

Purée the strawberries in an electric blender or rub through a sieve, then strain. Stir in the water and 25 g (1 oz) of the sugar and mix well.

Beat the egg yolks with the remaining sugar in a basin over a pan of hot water until thick and creamy. Fold in the cream and purée.

TO FREEZE: Pour into a rigid container, seal, label and freeze.

TO SERVE: Soften in the refrigerator about 1 hour before required.

Serves 6

Savarin

ENRICHED DOUGH:
275 g (9 oz) strong
    plain flour, sifted
pinch of salt
2 tablespoons caster
    sugar
25 g (1 oz) fresh
    yeast
300 ml (½ pint)
    warm milk
3 eggs, beaten
125 g (4 oz) butter,
    softened
TO SERVE:
125 g (4 oz) sugar
150 ml (¼ pint)
    water
strip of lemon rind
fresh fruit to taste
    (strawberries,
    raspberries,
    pineapple,
    peaches, etc.)

To make the dough, combine the flour, salt and sugar in a large bowl. Dissolve the yeast in the milk and add to the flour with the eggs. Beat for 5 minutes until smooth and begining to froth. Cover and leave to rise in a warm place for 1 hour.

Add the softened butter to the batter, in pieces. Beat with a wooden spoon for 5 minutes. Pour into a greased and floured 23 cm (9 inch) savarin mould and leave in a warm place for 10 minutes.

Bake in a preheated moderately hot oven, 200°C (400°F), Gas Mark 6, for 35 minutes, until well risen and golden. Cool on a wire rack.

TO FREEZE: Wrap the savarin in plastic wrap and then in a polythene bag. Seal, label and freeze.

TO SERVE: Thaw in the wrappings at room temperature for 2 hours, then unwrap and place on a serving dish.

Dissolve the sugar in the water over low heat. Add the lemon rind and boil for 5 minutes. Remove the rind, and spoon over the savarin.

Pile the fruit in the centre and serve with whipped cream.

Serves 6

Rum Babas

ENRICHED DOUGH:
275 g (9 oz) strong
  plain flour, sifted
pinch of salt
2 tablespoons caster
  sugar
25 g (1 oz) fresh
  yeast
300 ml (1/2 pint)
  warm milk
3 eggs, beaten
125 g (4 oz) butter,
  softened
50 g (2 oz) currants
TO SERVE:
125 g (4 oz) sugar
150 ml (1/4 pint)
  water
strip of lemon rind
2 tablespoons rum
300 ml (1/2 pint)
  whipping cream,
  whipped
6 glacé cherries

Make the dough as for Savarin (see opposite), adding the currants with the butter. Divide the mixture between six 10 cm (4 inch) baba moulds and leave in a warm place for 5 minutes.

Bake in a preheated moderately hot oven, 200°C (400°F), Gas Mark 6, for 15 to 20 minutes. Cool on a wire rack.

TO FREEZE: Pack in a rigid container. Seal, label and freeze.

TO SERVE: Thaw in the container at room temperature for 2 hours, then place on individual plates.

Make up the syrup as opposite, using rum instead of Kirsch. Fill each baba with whipped cream and decorate with a glacé cherry.

Serves 6

Profiteroles

CHOUX PASTRY:
150 ml (¼ pint) water
50 g (2 oz) butter
65 g (2½ oz) plain flour, sifted
2 eggs, beaten
TO SERVE:
300 ml (½ pint) double cream, whipped
Rich Chocolate Sauce (see page 16)

Make the choux pastry as for Savoury Ham Puffs (see page 62). Place heaped teaspoonfuls, well apart, on dampened baking sheets. Bake in a preheated moderately hot oven, 200°C (400°F), Gas Mark 6, for 20 minutes. Make a small slit in each one, then cool on a wire rack.

TO FREEZE: Pack in a rigid container. Seal, label and freeze.

TO SERVE: Place on baking sheets and thaw in a preheated moderate oven, 180°C (350°F), Gas Mark 4, for about 10 minutes. Cool on a wire rack.

Fill with cream, pile into a serving dish and pour over the sauce.
Serves 4

Rich Curd Cheesecake

500 g (1 lb) curd cheese, sieved
50 g (2 oz) butter
125 g (4 oz) caster sugar
1 egg, beaten
few drops of vanilla essence
175 g (6 oz) digestive biscuits, crumbed
TO SERVE:
250 g (8 oz) dried apricots
sugar
3 tablespoons apricot jam, warmed and sieved

Place the cheese in a bowl. Gradually beat in three quarters of the butter, the sugar and egg. Continue beating until light and fluffy. Add the vanilla essence.

Butter an 18 cm (7 inch) foil flan dish thickly with the remaining butter. Spread half the biscuit crumbs in the dish and spoon in the cheese mixture. Spread the rest of the crumbs on top and bake in a pre-heated moderate oven, 180°C (350°F), Gas Mark 4, for 25 minutes. Cool.

TO FREEZE: Open freeze, then place in a polythene bag. Seal, label and return to the freezer.

TO SERVE: Unwrap, transfer to a serving dish and thaw in the refrigerator for about 8 hours.

Soak the apricots in water to cover for at least 1 hour, then cook gently in the soaking liquid until soft. Add sugar to taste. Cool, then drain and arrange the apricots on the cheesecake. Brush jam over the fruit to glaze.
Serves 6

Lemon Pancakes

125 g (4 oz) plain
  flour
pinch of salt
1 egg
300 ml (½ pint)
  milk
oil
TO SERVE:
juice of 1 lemon
sugar to taste
lemon twists

Sift the flour and salt into a bowl. Add the egg and gradually beat in half the milk. Add the remaining milk and beat until smooth.

Lightly oil a frying pan and place over a moderate heat. Pour in just enough batter to cover the base of the pan. Cook until the underside is golden, then turn and cook the other side. Cool on a wire rack. Repeat with the remaining batter.

TO FREEZE: Stack the pancakes, with greaseproof paper between each one. Place the pile in a polythene bag. Seal, label and freeze.

TO SERVE: Thaw the wrapped pile at room temperature for 2 to 3 hours, or remove individual pancakes as needed and thaw for 15 to 20 minutes.

Unwrap the pile and reheat in a moderately hot oven, 190°C (375°F), Gas Mark 5, for 20 to 30 minutes. Reheat individual pancakes in a lightly greased hot frying pan for about 3 minutes on each side.

Sprinkle with lemon juice, roll up and top with sugar and lemon twists.
Makes 8 to 10 pancakes

Crêpes Suzette

175 g (6 oz) butter
175 g (6 oz) caster
  sugar
grated rind of 2
  oranges
juice of 1 orange
6 cooked pancakes,
  see above
TO SERVE:
15 g (½ oz) butter
4 tablespoons
  brandy, warmed

Cream the butter with the sugar. Beat in the orange rind and juice. Spread over the pancakes and fold each one into four.

TO FREEZE: Pack in a rigid container, with waxed paper between them. Seal, label and freeze.

TO SERVE: Unwrap and thaw at room temperature for about 30 minutes. Melt the butter in a frying pan. When foaming, add the crêpes, in a single layer. Cook for about 1 minute, turn and cook the other side. Pour over the brandy and ignite.
Serves 6

Baked Ginger Pudding with Rum Sauce

125 g (4 oz) butter
125 g (4 oz) caster
  sugar
2 eggs
125 g (4 oz) stem
  ginger, chopped
175 g (6 oz)
  self-raising flour,
  sifted
2 tablespoons milk
TO SERVE:
1 egg
1 egg yolk
25 g (1 oz) caster
  sugar
2 tablespoons rum

Cream the butter and sugar, then beat in the eggs one at a time. Stir in the chopped ginger.

Fold in the flour, then add the milk. Spoon into a greased foil pudding basin. Bake in a preheated moderately hot oven, 190°C (375°F), Gas Mark 5, for about 35 minutes until risen and golden. Cool.

TO FREEZE: Cover, place in a polythene bag, seal, label and freeze.

TO SERVE: Uncover and place in a preheated moderately hot oven, 190°C (375°F), Gas Mark 5, for 45 minutes.

Meanwhile, prepare the rum sauce. Put the egg, egg yolk, sugar and rum in a basin over a pan of hot water and whisk until the sauce is thick and frothy.

Turn the pudding on to a serving dish and pour over the sauce.

Serves 4

French Apple Flan

1 x 212 g (7½ oz)
    packet frozen
    shortcrust pastry,
    thawed
3-4 cooking apples,
    peeled and sliced
300 ml (½ pint)
    water
75 g (3 oz) sugar
    (approximately)
500 g (1 lb) dessert
    apples (e.g.
    Worcestershire
    Pearmain), sliced
TO SERVE:
3 tablespoons apricot
    jam, warmed and
    sieved

Roll out the pastry and use to line a
23 cm (9 inch) French fluted flan
ring. Bake blind in a preheated
moderately hot oven, 190°C (375°F),
Gas Mark 5, for 20 minutes. Cool.

Place the cooking apples in a pan
with 2 to 3 tablespoons of the water
and cook gently until pulped. Add
sugar to taste and cool.

Dissolve 4 tablespoons sugar in the
remaining water over low heat. Add
the dessert apples and poach gently
until they are just tender but still
retain their shape. Drain and cool.

Spread the apple pulp in the flan
case and arrange the apple slices in
circles on top.

TO FREEZE: Open freeze, then remove
the flan ring and wrap in foil. Seal,
label and return to the freezer.

TO SERVE: Replace the flan in its flan
ring. Reheat from frozen in a
preheated moderately hot oven,
190°C (375°F), Gas Mark 5, for 25
minutes. Brush the jam over the
apple slices. Serve with cream.
Serves 6

Raspberry and Redcurrant Flan

1 x 212 g (7½ oz)
    packet frozen
    shortcrust pastry,
    thawed
250 g (8 oz)
    redcurrants, topped
    and tailed
2 tablespoons sugar
300 ml (½ pint)
    water
2 teaspoons arrowroot
350 g (12 oz)
    raspberries
TO SERVE:
3 tablespoons
    redcurrant jelly

Prepare and bake the pastry case as
for French Apple Flan (see above).

Place the redcurrants in a pan. Add
the sugar and water and cook gently
for 10 minutes, until just tender.

Dissolve the arrowroot in a little
water and stir into the redcurrants.
Mix in the raspberries and spoon
into the flan case.

TO FREEZE: Freeze as for French
Apple Flan (see above).

TO SERVE: Unwrap and thaw at room
temperature for about 2 hours.
Warm the redcurrant jelly and brush
over the fruit. Serve with cream.
Serves 6

Plum Sorbet

1 kg (2 lb) plums,
    stoned
250 g (8 oz) sugar
300 ml (½ pint)
    water
15 g (½ oz) gelatine
½ egg white,
    whisked

Place the plums, 50 g (2 oz) of the sugar and the water in a saucepan and cook until soft. Strain, reserving the cooking liquid, and purée in an electric blender or rub through a sieve. Strain to remove skins, if necessary.

Dissolve the remaining sugar in the cooking liquid over low heat, then boil rapidly for 5 minutes; cool. Dissolve the gelatine in 5 tablespoons of the syrup in a bowl over a pan of hot water. Stir the dissolved gelatine and remaining syrup into the plum purée.

TO FREEZE: Pour into a rigid polythene container and freeze for about 1 hour. Whisk to break down the ice crystals, then fold in the egg white. Return to the container. Seal, label and freeze.

TO SERVE: Transfer to the refrigerator about 1 hour before required to soften slightly.

Serves 6

Strawberry Mousse with Raspberry Sauce

250 g (8 oz) fresh or
    frozen strawberries
3 eggs, separated
50 g (2 oz) caster
    sugar
15 g (½ oz) gelatine
5 tablespoons water
150 ml (¼ pint)
    double cream
TO SERVE:
250 g (8 oz) fresh or
    frozen raspberries,
    thawed
2-3 tablespoons caster
    sugar

Make as for Bramble Mousse (opposite), replacing the blackberries with strawberries. Pour into a foil dish and chill.

TO FREEZE: Cover, place in a polythene bag, seal, label and freeze.

TO SERVE: Thaw, covered, at room temperature for 5 to 6 hours. Purée the raspberries in an electric blender or rub through a sieve, then strain to remove pips, if necessary. Add sugar to taste, then spoon over the mousse.

Serves 4 to 6

Bramble Mousse

*250 g (8 oz) fresh or
   frozen blackberries*
3 eggs, separated
*50 g (2 oz) caster
   sugar*
15 g (½ oz) gelatine
5 tablespoons water
*150 ml (¼ pint)
   double cream*
TO SERVE:
*150 ml (¼ pint)
   double cream*

Purée the blackberries in an electric
blender or rub through a sieve, then
strain to remove pips, if necessary.
Whisk the egg yolks and sugar
together until thick and creamy.

Dissolve the gelatine in the water
in a bowl over a pan of hot water.
Cool, then fold into the egg yolk
mixture.

Whisk the egg whites until stiff.
Whip the cream lightly. Fold the egg
whites and cream into the egg yolk
mixture. Pour into a foil dish and
chill.

TO FREEZE: Cover, place in a
polythene bag, seal, label and freeze.
TO SERVE: Thaw, covered, at room
temperature for 5 to 6 hours.
Decorate with whipped cream.
Serves 4 to 6

BAKING

Chocolate Feather Gâteau

4 eggs
125 g (4 oz) caster
sugar
75 g (3 oz)
self-raising flour
25 g (1 oz) cocoa
TO SERVE:
450 ml (³/4 pint)
double cream,
whipped
2 tablespoons icing
sugar, sifted

Whisk together the eggs and sugar until pale and thick. Sift together the flour and cocoa and lightly fold into the eggs. Divide between two greased and floured 20 cm (8 inch) sandwich tins.

Bake in a preheated moderately hot oven, 190°C (375°F), Gas Mark 5, for about 20 minutes, until well risen and just firm to the touch. Turn onto a wire rack to cool.

TO FREEZE: Place the cakes one on top of the other with greaseproof paper between them. Place in a polythene bag, seal, label and freeze.

TO SERVE: Thaw, wrapped, at room temperature for 1 hour. Cut each cake in half horizontally. Sandwich the layers together with the cream and sprinkle the top with icing sugar.

Makes one 20 cm (8 inch) gâteau

Mixed Fruit Cake

250 g (8 oz)
  self-raising flour
pinch of salt
250 g (8 oz) butter
250 g (8 oz) caster
  sugar
grated rind of 1 small
  orange
4 eggs, beaten
50 g (2 oz) ground
  almonds
125 g (4 oz) currants
125 g (4 oz)
  sultanas
125 g (4 oz) raisins
25 g (1 oz) chopped
  mixed peel
125 g (4 oz) glacé
  cherries, chopped

Sift the flour and salt together.

Cream the butter, sugar and orange rind until light and fluffy. Gradually beat in the eggs, adding a little flour. Fold in the remaining ingredients, with the flour.

Turn into a lined and greased 20 cm (8 inch) round deep cake tin and smooth the top. Bake in a preheated moderate oven, 160°C (325°F), Gas Mark 3, for about 2½ hours, until a skewer inserted in the centre comes out clean.

Leave in the tin for 10 minutes, then turn onto a wire rack to cool; remove the paper.

TO FREEZE: Wrap in foil, seal, label and freeze.

TO SERVE: Thaw, wrapped, for 6 hours at room temperature.

Makes one 20 cm (8 inch) round cake

Marbled Ring Cake

4 large eggs
125 g (4 oz) caster
  sugar
125 g (4 oz)
  self-raising flour,
  sifted
1 tablespoon cocoa
CHOCOLATE BUTTER
  CREAM:
125 g (4 oz) butter
250 g (8 oz) icing
  sugar, sifted
75 g (3 oz)
  chocolate, melted

Whisk the eggs and sugar together until thick and pale. Transfer half the mixture into another bowl.

Fold half the flour into one portion of the mixture. Sift the cocoa with the remaining flour and fold into the other portion. Spoon the dark and light mixtures alternately into a greased and floured 23 cm (9 inch) ring tin.

Bake in a preheated moderately hot oven, 190°C (375°F), Gas Mark 5, for 25 minutes, until well risen and just beginning to shrink from the side of the tin. Turn onto a wire rack to cool.

TO FREEZE: Place in a polythene bag, seal, label and freeze.

TO SERVE: Unwrap and thaw at room temperature for about 2 hours.

Meanwhile, make the buttercream. Cream together the butter and icing sugar, then beat in the chocolate. Spread over the cake, with a palette knife.

Makes one 23 cm (9 inch) cake

Coffee and Walnut Gâteau

175 g (6 oz) butter
175 g (6 oz) caster
   sugar
3 eggs, beaten
2 tablespoons instant
   coffee powder,
   dissolved in 2
   tablespoons water
150 g (5 oz)
   self-raising flour,
   sifted
COFFEE BUTTERCREAM:
350 g (12 oz) butter
625 g (1¼ lb) icing
   sugar, sifted
1 tablespoon instant
   coffee powder,
   dissolved in 1
   tablespoon water
TO DECORATE:
4 tablespoons
   chopped walnuts
12 walnut halves

Cream the butter and sugar until soft and light. Gradually beat in the eggs, then the coffee. Fold in the flour. Divide between two 20 cm (8 inch) greased and floured sandwich tins.

Bake in a preheated moderately hot oven, 190°C (375°F), Gas Mark 5, for 25 minutes, until well risen and just firm to the touch. Turn onto a wire rack to cool.

To prepare the buttercream, beat the butter until soft, then gradually beat in the icing sugar alternately with the coffee. Beat until smooth.

Sandwich the cake layers together with one quarter of the buttercream. Spread another quarter around the sides and roll in the chopped nuts. Cover the top with more buttercream. Decorate with walnut halves.
TO FREEZE: Put the cake on a cardboard plate and freeze uncovered, then wrap carefully in plastic wrap and put in a rigid box. Seal, label and return to the freezer.
TO SERVE: Unwrap and thaw at room temperature for about 4 hours.
Makes on 20 cm (8 inch) gâteau

American Apple Cake

125 g (4 oz) butter
350 g (12 oz) caster
  sugar
2 eggs, beaten
250 g (8 oz) plain
  flour
1 teaspoon
  bicarbonate of soda
1 tablespoon ground
  cinnamon
1 ½ teaspoons ground
  nutmeg
1 teaspoon salt
750 g (1 ½ lb)
  apples, peeled and
  finely chopped
125 g (4 oz)
  chopped mixed
  nuts

Cream together the butter and sugar, then gradually beat in the eggs. Sift the flour, soda, spices and salt together and fold into the creamed mixture, then fold in the apples and nuts.

Turn into a greased tin, about 23 x 33 cm (9 x 13 inches). Bake in a preheated moderate oven, 180°C (350°F), Gas Mark 4, for 1¼ hours, then lower the temperature to 150°C (300°F), Gas Mark 2, and cook for 45 minutes. Cool in the tin.

TO FREEZE: Remove the tin, wrap in foil and place in a polythene bag. Seal, label and freeze.

TO SERVE: Thaw, wrapped, at room temperature for 2 hours. Cut into squares.

**Makes one 23 x 33 cm
(9 x 13 inch) cake**

Date and Ginger Buns

175 g (6 oz)
  self-raising flour
pinch of salt
1 teaspoon ground
  ginger
75 g (3 oz) butter or
  margarine
75 g (3 oz) light
  brown sugar
75 g (3 oz) stoned
  dates, chopped
1 egg, beaten
milk to mix

Sift the flour, salt and ginger together into a bowl. Rub in the fat until the mixture resembles breadcrumbs. Stir in the sugar and dates, then mix in the egg and enough milk to give a dropping consistency. Divide between 18 greased bun tins.

Bake in a preheated moderately hot oven, 190°C (375°F), Gas Mark 5, for 15 minutes until golden and firm to touch. Turn onto a wire rack to cool.

TO FREEZE: Open freeze, then place in a rigid container, with greaseproof paper between the layers. Cover, seal, label and return to the freezer.

TO SERVE: Unwrap and thaw at room temperature for 1 hour.

Makes 18

Almond Shortbread

125 g (4 oz) butter
50 g (2 oz) soft
  brown sugar
½ egg yolk
250 g (8 oz)
  wholewheat flour
pinch of salt
25 g (1 oz) ground
  almonds
TO SERVE:
caster sugar

Cream together the butter and sugar and beat in the egg yolk. Mix in the flour and salt, then add the almonds and knead lightly until evenly distributed. Press into a 20 cm (8 inch) sandwich tin and prick all over with a fork. Bake in a preheated cool oven, 150°C (300°F), Gas Mark 2, for about 50 minutes. Turn onto a wire rack to cool.

TO FREEZE: Wrap in plastic wrap and pack in a rigid box. Seal, label and freeze.

TO SERVE: Unwrap and thaw at room temperature for 1 hour. Sprinkle with caster sugar and cut into wedges.

Makes 8

Nutty Date Slices

250 g (8 oz) stoned
  dates, chopped
2 tablespoons water
1 tablespoon lemon
  juice
1 tablespoon honey
50 g (2 oz) walnuts
125 g (4 oz)
  wholewheat flour
175 g (6 oz) rolled
  oats
250 g (8 oz) butter

Place the dates, water, lemon juice
and honey in a pan and simmer until
the dates are soft. Stir in the walnuts
then cool.

Mix the flour with the oats and
rub in the butter. Work to a dough,
then knead lightly on a floured
surface. Press half the dough into a
greased 18 cm (7 inch) square cake
tin. Spread the date mixture over the
top and cover with the remaining
dough.

Bake in a preheated moderate
oven, 180°C (350°F), Gas Mark 4, for
25 minutes. Cool slightly, then cut
into squares. Leave to cool
completely before removing from
the tin.

TO FREEZE: Pack in a polythene bag,
seal, label and freeze.

TO SERVE: Unwrap and thaw at room
temperature for about 2 hours.
Makes 16

Wholewheat Bread

1.5 kg (3 lb)
  wholewheat flour
25 g (1 oz) salt
25 g (1 oz) lard
40 g (1½ oz) fresh
  yeast
900 ml (1½ pints)
  warm water

Mix together the flour and salt and rub in the lard. Blend the yeast with the water, add to the flour and mix to a dough. Turn onto a floured surface and knead for 10 minutes. Place in a greased bowl, cover with oiled plastic wrap and leave to rise in a warm place for about 1 hour until doubled in size.

Turn out and knead for 1 minute, then cut into four. Shape into oblongs and place in greased 500 g (1 lb) loaf tins. Cover and leave in a warm place for about 1 hour until risen to the top of the tins.

Bake in a preheated hot oven, 230°C (450°F), Gas Mark 8, for about 40 minutes until the bread sounds hollow when tapped on the bottom. Turn onto a wire rack to cool.

TO FREEZE: Place in polythene bags, seal, label and freeze.

TO SERVE: Thaw, wrapped, at room temperature for about 4 hours.

Makes 4 x 500 g (1 lb) loaves

Muffins

750 g (1½ lb) strong
  plain flour
1 teaspoon salt
25 g (1 oz) fresh
  yeast
450 ml (¾ pint)
  warm milk
TO SERVE:
butter

Sift the flour and salt together. Blend the yeast into the milk, add to the flour and mix to a soft dough. Cover and leave to rise in a warm place for about 1 hour.

Turn onto a floured surface and divide into 12 equal pieces. Pat each piece into a circle and place in greased 10 cm (4 inch) muffin rings on baking sheets. Bake in a preheated moderately hot oven, 190°C (375°F), Gas Mark 5, for 25 minutes. Turn onto a wire rack to cool.

TO FREEZE: Pack in a polythene bag, seal, label and freeze.

TO SERVE: Toast the frozen muffins on both sides, pull apart and butter thickly.

Makes 12

Hot Cross Buns

500 g (1 lb) strong
  plain flour
1/2 teaspoon salt
1 teaspoon ground
  mixed spice
25 g (1 oz) fresh
  yeast
300 ml (1/2 pint)
  warm milk
75 g (3 oz) butter,
  melted
2 eggs, beaten
50 g (2 oz) caster
  sugar
175 g (6 oz) currants
50 g (2 oz)
  shortcrust pastry
  trimmings
  (approximately)
GLAZE:
1 teaspoon caster
  sugar
4 tablespoons milk

Sift the flour, salt and spice together.
Dissolve the yeast in the milk and
stir in the butter, eggs and sugar.
Add to the flour and beat to a
smooth dough. Turn onto a floured
surface and knead in the currants.
Knead for 10 minutes.

Place in a bowl, cover with a piece
of oiled plastic wrap and leave to rise
in a warm place for 1 hour. Turn out
and knead for 1 minute. Cover and
leave for 30 minutes. Divide into 18
pieces and shape into buns. Place on
greased baking sheets.

Roll out the pastry thinly and cut
into narrow strips. Brush with water
and place a pastry cross on each bun.
Leave in a warm place for 15 minutes.

Dissolve the sugar in the milk over
low heat and brush over the buns.

Bake in a preheated hot oven, 220°C
(425°F), Gas Mark 7, for about 15 minutes.
Turn onto a wire rack to cool.

TO FREEZE: Pack in a polythene bag,
seal, label and freeze.

TO SERVE: Unwrap, place on baking
sheets and thaw in a preheated
moderately hot oven, 190°C (375°F),
Gas Mark 5, for 15 minutes.

Makes 18

Vegetable Freezing Chart

When preparing vegetables for the freezer, blanch no more than 500 g (1 lb) at a time. Put the prepared vegetables in a blanching basket and lower into a large pan of boiling water. Time the blanching from the point at which the water returns to a fast boil. After blanching, immerse the vegetables in iced water to cool quickly, then drain and dry thoroughly.

Storage Time	Preparation and Packing	Thawing
Artichoke, Globe 6 months	Blanch with lemon juice added, for 7 to 10 minutes according to size. Pack in polythene bags.	Thaw in wrappings for 4 hours. Use as fresh.
Asparagus 9 months	Grade into thin and thick stems. Blanch thin stems for 2 minutes, thicker stems for 3 minutes. Tie in small bundles and pack in polythene bags.	Unwrap and thaw until easy to separate, then boil 2 to 3 minutes.
Aubergines 12 months	Cut into thick slices and blanch for 3 minutes. Pack in small portions in polythene bags. Or freeze in ratatouille.	Thaw in wrappings; pat dry before cooking.
Beans, Broad 12 months	Blanch for 2 minutes. Open freeze on trays and pack in polythene bags.	Boil from frozen for 3 to 5 minutes, according to size.
Beans, French 12 months	Blanch for 2 minutes. Open freeze on trays and pack in polythene bags.	Boil from frozen for 5 to 7 minutes, according to size.
Beans, Runner 12 months	Blanch for 2 minutes. Open freeze on trays and pack in polythene bags.	Boil from frozen for 5 to 7 minutes, according to size.
Beetroot 6 months	Cook as usual, slice and pack in rigid containers.	Thaw in containers in refrigerator, or unwrap and thaw at room temperature.
Broccoli 12 months	Grade into stem sizes. Blanch thin stems for 2 minutes, and thick stems for 4 minutes. Pack in small portions in polythene bags.	Boil from frozen for 3 to 7 minutes, according to size.
Brussels Sprouts 12 months	Blanch for 2 minutes. Open freeze on trays and pack in polythene bags.	Boil from frozen for 4 to 8 minutes.
Cabbage 6 months	Shred inner leaves, blanch for 1 minute. Or freeze in dishes such as Braised Cabbage.	Boil from frozen for 5 to 8 minutes.
Carrots 9 months	Blanch whole young carrots for 2 minutes, thinly slice older ones and blanch for 5 minutes. Open freeze on trays and pack in polythene bags.	Boil from frozen for 4 minutes.

Storage Time	Preparation and Packing	Thawing
Cauliflower 6 months	Break into florets and blanch for 3 minutes. Pack in portions in polythene bags.	Boil from frozen for 5 minutes.
Corn 12 months	Remove husks and silks and blanch cobs for 5 minutes. Pack in polythene bags. Alternatively strip off kernels and pack in portions.	Thaw cobs in wrappings for 2 hours, then boil for 5 to 10 minutes. Toss frozen kernels in butter to heat only.
Courgettes 6 months	Slice thickly. Sauté in butter for 1 minute and pack in portions in foil dishes. Or blanch for 2 minutes and pack in polythene bags.	Thaw in dishes and heat gently. Boil blanched ones from frozen for 4 minutes.
Leeks 6 months	Blanch for 3 minutes and pack in freezer bags.	Boil from frozen for 6 to 8 minutes.
Marrow 6 months	Freeze as ratatouille or other cooked dish. Or cut into 5 cm (2 inch) rings, blanch for 5 minutes and pack in rigid containers.	Steam, uncovered, from frozen for 1 to 2 minutes.
Mushrooms 3 months	Sauté lightly in butter and pack in portions in foil dishes, or freeze in cooked dishes e.g. soup, casseroles.	Thaw in wrappings for 2 hours and add to dishes.
Onions	Chop and blanch for 2 minutes. Pack in small portions in polythene bags. Blanch tiny onions whole for 3 minutes and open freeze on trays.	Add whole or chopped frozen onions to required sauce, casserole or soup.
Parsnips 6 months	Slice thinly and blanch for 2 minutes. Pack in portions in polythene bags.	Boil from frozen for 10 to 15 minutes.
Peas 12 months	Blanch for 1 minute. Open freeze on trays and pack in polythene bags.	Boil from frozen for 4 minutes.
Peppers 12 months	Chop or leave whole and blanch for 2 minutes. Pack in small portions for use in cooked dishes.	Thaw in wrappings for 1 to 2 hours.
Potatoes 3 months	Freeze partially cooked for chips: Deep-fry for 2 to 3 minutes. Cool and pack in polythene bags.	Unwrap and thaw. Refry for 3 to 4 minutes.
Spinach 12 months	Blanch for 2 minutes, drain well and pack in portions in polythene bags.	Boil from frozen for about 5 minutes.
Tomatoes 12 months	Pack whole in small quantities in polythene bags. Or freeze as purée: Simmer chopped tomatoes until soft, then sieve, season and cook until reduced. Pack in rigid containers.	Thaw whole tomatoes in wrappings for 2 hours; use in cooked dishes. Thaw purée in containers.

INDEX